COME HOME
to Crochet
- BY KNIT PICKS -

Copyright 2018 © Knit Picks

All rights reserved. This book or any portion thereof may not be reproduced or used in any manner whatsoever without the express written permission of the publisher except for the use of brief quotations in a book review.

Photography by Amy Setter

Printed in the United States of America

First Printing, 2018

ISBN 978-1-62767-201-6

Versa Press, Inc

800-447-7829

www.versapress.com

CONTENTS

Daisy Chain	**7**
Darling Dinner Set	**11**
Housewarming Pillow	**17**
Mandala Pillow	**21**
Serenity Afghan	**25**
Tidepool Placemat	**31**
Woven Blanket	**35**

Is there anything more deeply soul quenching than spending time in one's own space, immersed in the task of creating beautiful things?

A pillow to rest your weary head after long day. A soft chunky blanket to cozy up under on a rainy afternoon. For some, it truly doesn't get any better than this simple joy.

Boasting sumptuous textures and soothing colors, this collection is full of ideas and inspiration that will have you creating plush textiles for every nook in your house. You'll look forward to the end of every day when you can come to home to crochet.

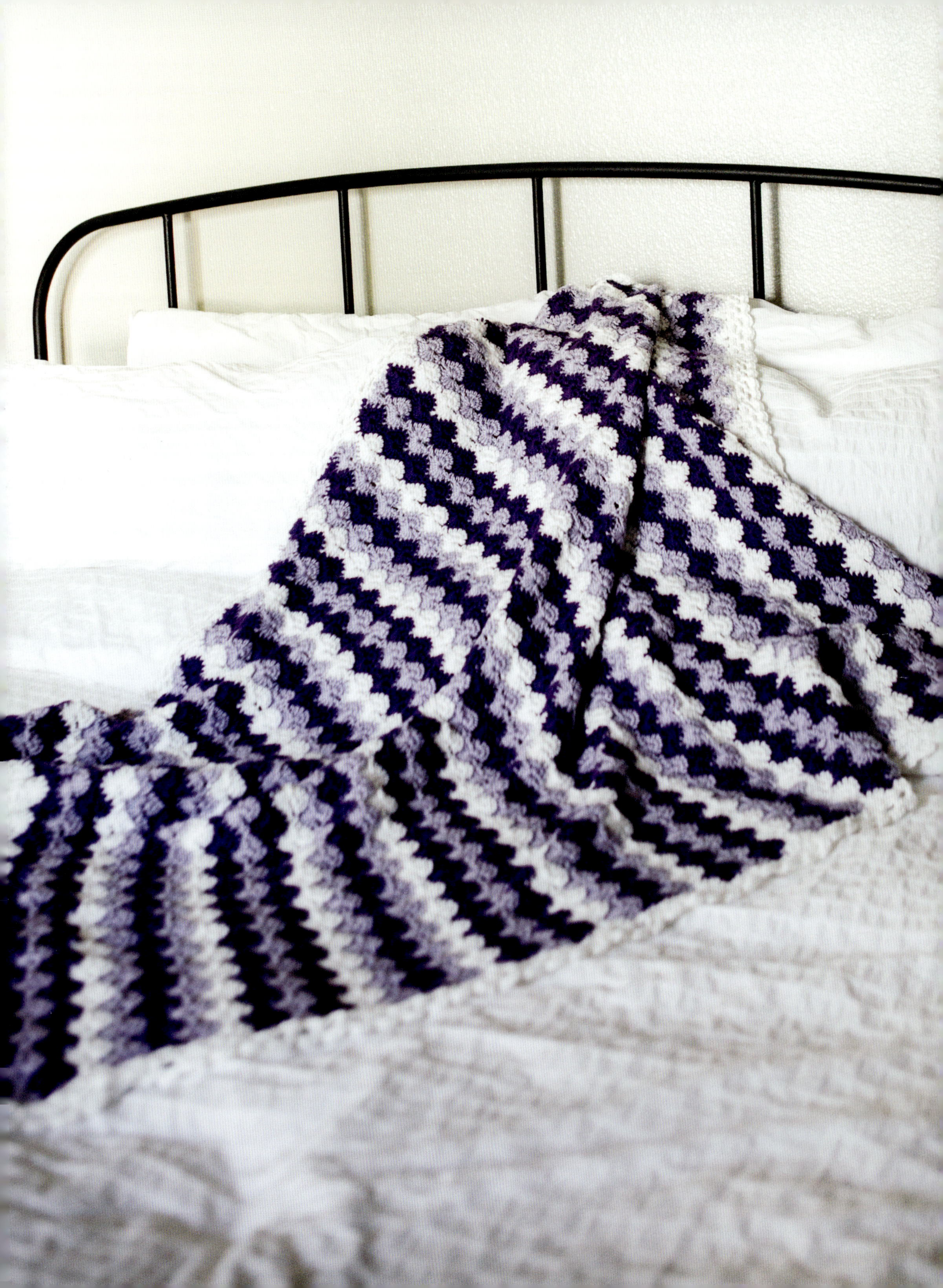

DAISY CHAIN

by Kristen Stoltzfus Clay

FINISHED MEASUREMENTS
39 x 50"

YARN
Knit Picks Shine Sport
(60% Pima Cotton, 40% Modal®; 110 yards/50g): C1 White 24486, 6 balls; C2 Wisteria 25333, C3 Iris 24789, 7 balls each.

HOOKS
US G/6 (4.00 mm)

NOTIONS
Yarn Needle

GAUGE
3 shells and 4 sc = 4.5"

8 rows = 4"

For pattern support, contact
joysinstitches@outlook.com

Notes:
Cartwheels of color interweave like flower chains in an all-over stripe effect surrounded with a simple lace edging for a combination to keep cozy in style and add arresting colorplay to any room. The stitch pattern is created in two parts using cluster stitches and shells.

Shell: 7 DC in specified st
Cluster (cl): (YO, insert hook in next st, draw up a lp, draw new lp through 2 lps on hook) 7 times, draw new lp through all 8 lps on hook.
Beginning Half Cluster (beg half cl): (YO, insert hook in next st, draw up a lp, draw new lp through 2 lps on hook) 3 times, draw new lp through all 4 lps on hook.
Half Cluster (half cl): (YO, insert hook in next st, draw up a lp, draw new lp through 2 lps on hook) 4 times, draw new lp through all 5 lps on hook.

Pattern Notes
First ch 3 counts as first dc throughout.
Cluster stitches are worked over 3 dc of one shell, the sc between, and 3 dc of next shell.

DIRECTIONS
With C1, ch 154.
Row 1: WS Work 3 DC in 4th ch from hook, (SK next 2 chs, SC in next ch, SK next 2 chs, work Shell in next ch) across, ending with SK next 2 chs, SC in next ch, SK next 2 chs, work 4 DC in last ch, fasten off C1. 24 shells
Row 2: With WS facing, join C2 in first dc, ch 1, SC in first dc, (ch 3, work CL, ch 3, SC in next (center) st of shell) across, ending with SC in last dc, ch 1, turn. 25 cl
Row 3: Ch 1, SC in first sc, (work Shell in cl, SC in next sc) across, fasten off C2. 25 shells
Row 4: With RS facing, join C3 in first sc, ch 3, work Beg Half CL, (ch 3, SC in next (center) st of shell, ch 3, work CL) across, ending with ch 3, SC in next (center) st of shell, ch 3, work Half CL, ch 3, turn. 24 cl, 2 half cl
Row 5: Work 3 DC in half cl, SC in next sc, (Shell in next cl, SC in next sc) across, ending with 4 DC in last half cl, fasten off C3. 24 shells
Rows 6-7: Rep Rows 2-3.
Rows 8-9: With C1, rep Rows 4-5.
Rows 10-11: With C3, rep Rows 2-3.
Rows 12-13: With C2, rep Rows 4-5.
Rows 14-15: With C3, rep Rows 2-3
Rows 16-17: With C1, rep Rows 4-5.
Rows 18-96: Rep Rows 2-17 4 times, rep Rows 2-16 once more, turn to work with RS facing.

Edging
Rnd 1: (Work 150 SC evenly along short side, work 3 SC in corner, work 198 SC evenly along long side, work 3 SC in corner) twice, join with Sl St in first sc. 708 sc
Rnd 2: Sl St into next st, (ch 1, SC) in first st, *ch 3, (SK 2 sc, SC in next sc, ch 3) across to corner, (SC, ch 3, SC) in corner sc; rep from * around, ch 3, SK last 2 sc, Sl St in last sc, join with Sl St in first sc.
Rnd 3: Sl St into next ch-sp, (ch 1, SC) in first ch-sp, *(ch 3, SC in next ch-sp) across to corner, in corner ch-sp work (2 HDC, ch 2, 2 HDC), SC in next ch-sp; rep from * around, ch 3, join with Sl St in first sc.
Rnd 4: Work (SC, HDC, ch 1, HDC, SC) in each ch-sp around, working (3 DC, ch 2, 3 DC) in each corner sp, join with Sl St in first sc. Fasten off.

Finishing
Weave in ends, wash and block to diagram.

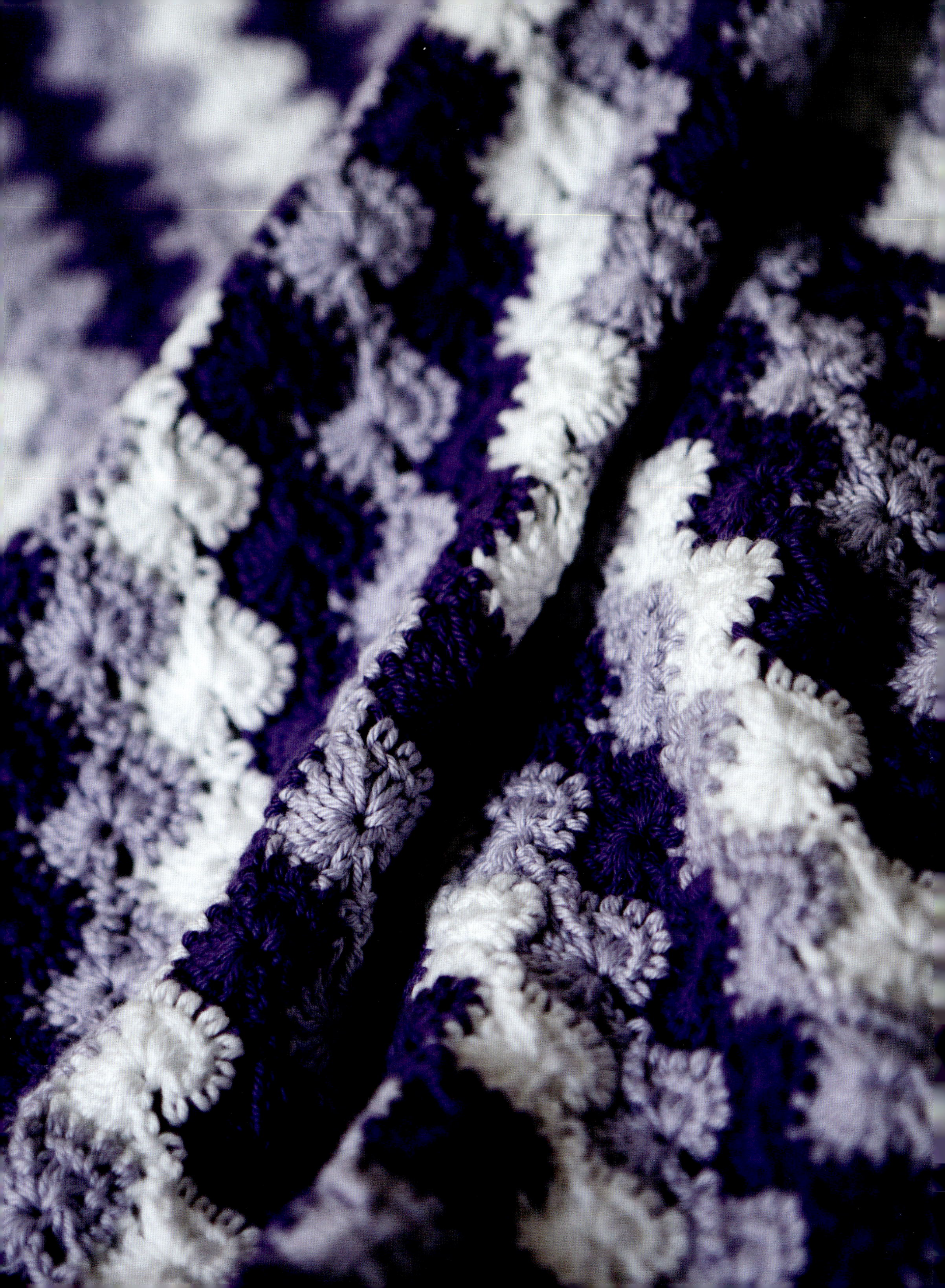

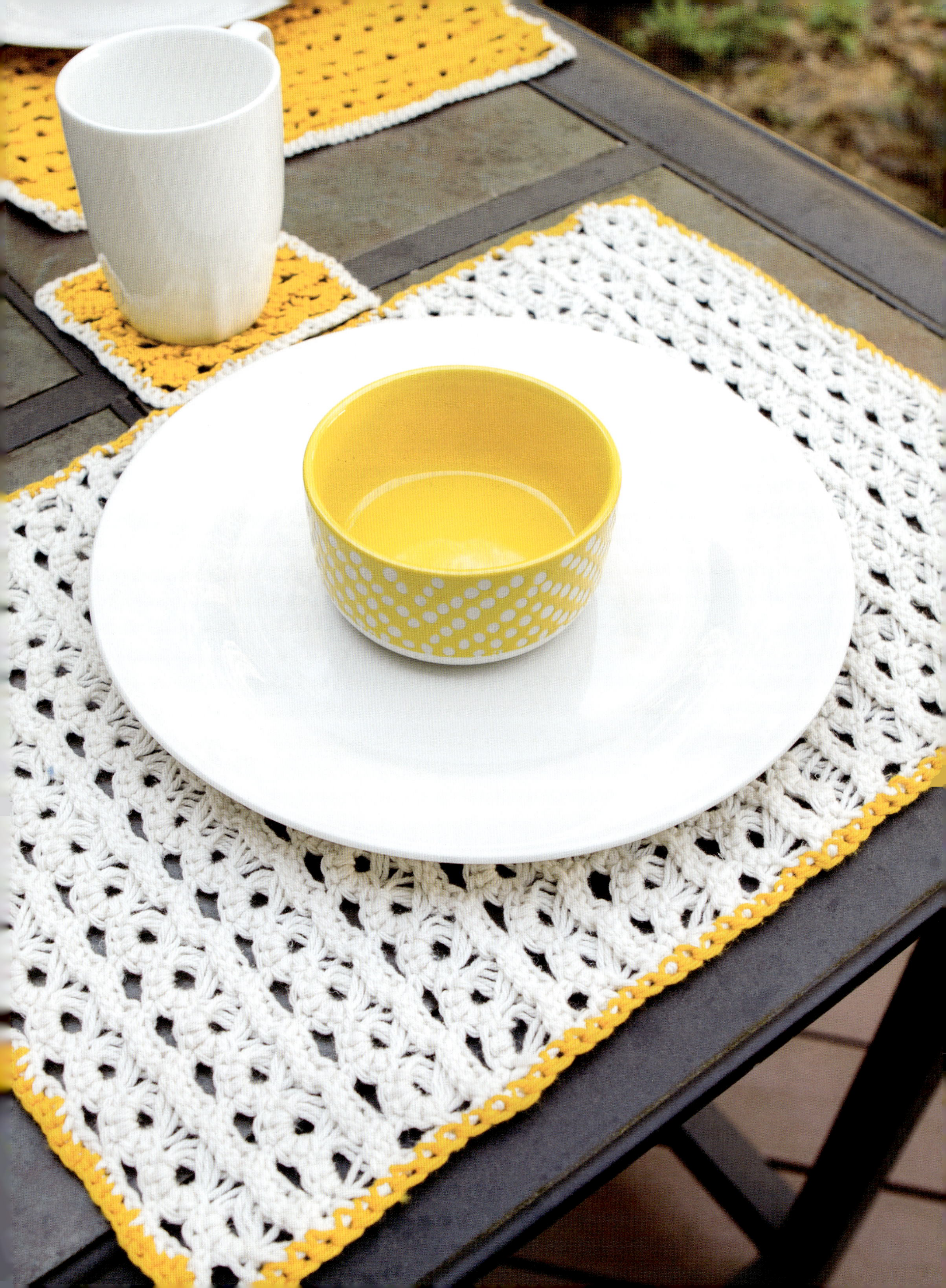

DARLING DINNER SET
by Kristi Simpson

FINISHED MEASUREMENTS
Placemat: 12 x 18"
Coaster: 4 x 4"

YARN
Knit Picks CotLin
(70% Tanguis Cotton, 30% Linen; 123 yards/50g): C1 Swan 24134, C2 Canary 24837, 1 ball each.

NEEDLES/HOOKS
US (15.00 mm) straight knitting needle.

US G/6 (4.00 mm) Crochet Hook

NOTIONS
Yarn Needle
Stitch Markers

GAUGE
4 sts x 1 row in broomstick lace = 4", blocked.

For pattern support, contact
kristi.rakj@gmail.com

Notes:
This set will decorate your table with elegance and flair. It is a mix of beautiful lace and functionality.

DIRECTIONS

Placemat
Using C1, ch 62.

Row 1: SC in second ch from hook, *ch 4, SK 3, SC in next ch; repeat from * across, SC in last ch.
Row 2: Working from left to right, slip last loop on hook onto knitting needle, SK first st, *working into the ch-4 sp, with hook pull up loop through ch and place on needle, SK sc st; repeat from * across, pull up loop in the last st, do not turn, pull first loop off needle, insert hook in loop, YO, pull through, YO, pull through (chain made), **insert hook in next 4 loops, 5 SC in 4-loop group; repeat from ** across to last loop, SC in last loop, turn.
Row 3: Ch 5, SC in 3rd sc of 5-sc group, *ch 4, SC in 3rd sc of next 5-sc group; repeat from * across, ch 2, DC in last st, turn.
Row 4: Ch 1, SC in first st, Sl St 2 in ch-sp, SC in next st, *Sl St 4 in each ch, SC in next st; repeat from * across to last sc, Sl St 2, SC in last st.
Row 5: Working from left to right, slip last loop on hook onto knitting needle, pull up loop in next 2 sl sts, SK sc, *working into the 4 sl st, with hook pull up loop and place on needle, SK sc; repeat from * across, pull up loop in the last 2 sl st, and last st, do not turn, insert hook in next 2 loops, 3 SC in 2-lp group, **insert hook in next 4 loops, 5 SC in 4-lp group; repeat from ** to last 3 loops, insert hook in next 2 loops, 3 SC in 2-lp group, SC in last loop, turn.
Row 6: Ch 1, SC 2, *ch 4, SC in 3rd sc of 5 sc group; repeat from * across to last 5-sc group, ch 4, SC in last 2 sts, turn.
Row 7: Ch 1, SC in first st, SC in next st, *Sl St in next 4 chs, SC in next sc; repeat across to last sc after ch-4 section, Sl St 4, SC in last 2 sts.
Row 8: Working from left to right, slip last loop on hook onto knitting needle, SK first st, *working into the ch-4 sp, with hook pull up loop through sl st and place on needle, SK sc; repeat from * across, pull up loop in the last st, do not turn, pull first loop off needle, insert hook in loop, YO, pull through, YO, pull through (chain made), **insert hook in next 4 loops, 5 SC in 4-loop group; repeat from ** across to last loop, SC in last loop, turn.
Rows 9-38: Repeat Rows 3-8. Fasten off.

Border
Use C2 to add border.
Working in ends of rows and stitches, ch 1, evenly SC down edge around with 3 SC in each corner, Sl St to the first st to join.

Coaster
Using C1, ch 22.

Row 1: SC in second ch from hook, *ch 4, SK 3, SC in next ch; repeat from * across, SC in last ch, turn.
Row 2: Working from left to right, slip last loop on hook onto knitting needle, SK first st, *working into ch-4 sp, with hook pull up loop through ch and place on needle, SK sc; repeat from * across, pull up loop in the last st, do not turn, pull first loop off needle, insert hook in loop, YO, pull through, YO, pull through (chain made), **insert hook in next 4 loops, 5 SC in 4-loop group; repeat from ** across to last loop, SC in last loop, turn.
Row 3: Ch 5, SC in 3rd sc of 5-sc group, *ch 4, SC in 3rd sc of next 5-sc group; repeat from * across, ch 2, DC in last st, turn.
Row 4: Ch 1, SC in first st, Sl St 2 in ch-sp, SC in next st, *Sl St 4 in each ch, SC in next st; repeat from * across to last sc, Sl St 2, SC in last st.
Row 5: Working from left to right, slip last loop on hook onto knitting needle, pull up loop in next 2 sl st, SK sc, *working into the 4 sl st, with hook pull up loop and place on needle, SK sc; repeat from * across, pull up loop in the last 2 sl st, and last st, do not turn, insert hook in next 2 loops, 3 SC in 2-lp group, ** insert hook in next 4 loops, 5 SC in 4-lp group; repeat from ** to last 3 loops, insert hook in next 2 loops, 3 SC in 2-lp group, SC in last loop, turn.
Row 6: Ch 1, SC 2, *ch 4, SC in 3rd sc of 5 sc group; repeat from * across to last 5-sc group, ch 4, SC in last 2 sts, turn.
Row 7: Ch 1, SC in first st, SC in next st, *Sl St in next 4 chs, SC in next sc; repeat across to last sc after ch-4 section, Sl St 4, SC in last 2 sts.
Row 8: Working from left to right, slip last loop on hook onto knitting needle, SK first st, *working into the ch-4 sp, with hook pull up loop through sl st and place on needle, SK sc; repeat from * across, pull up loop in the last st, do not turn, pull first loop off needle, insert hook in loop, YO, pull through, YO, pull through (chain made), **insert hook in next 4 loops, 5 SC in 4-loop group; repeat from ** across to last loop, SC in last loop, turn.
Row 9: Repeat Row 3. Fasten off.

Border
Use C2 to add border.
Working in ends of rows and stitches, ch 1, evenly SC down edge around with 3 SC in each corner, Sl St to the first st to join.

Finishing
Weave in ends, wash and block to measurements.

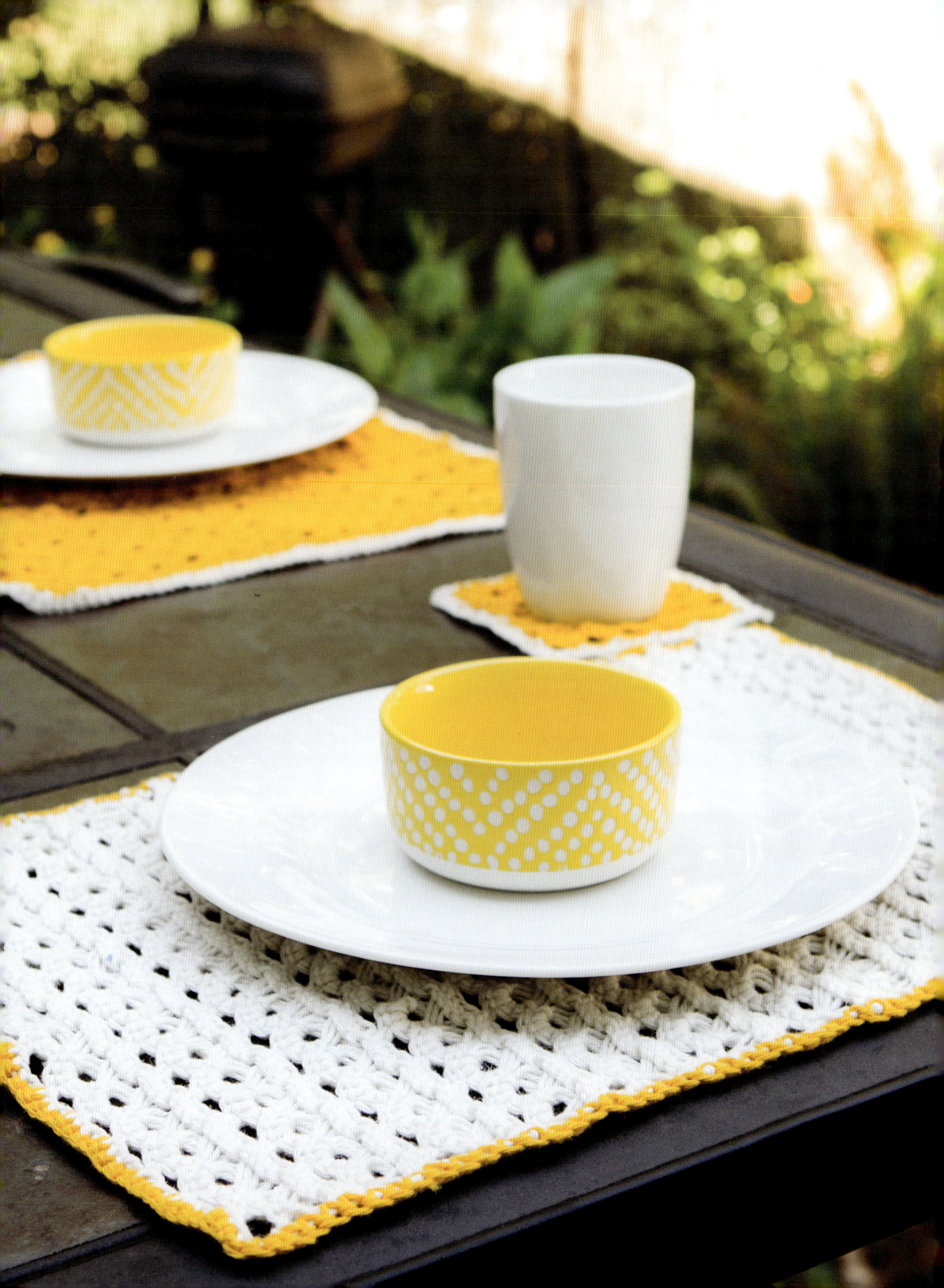

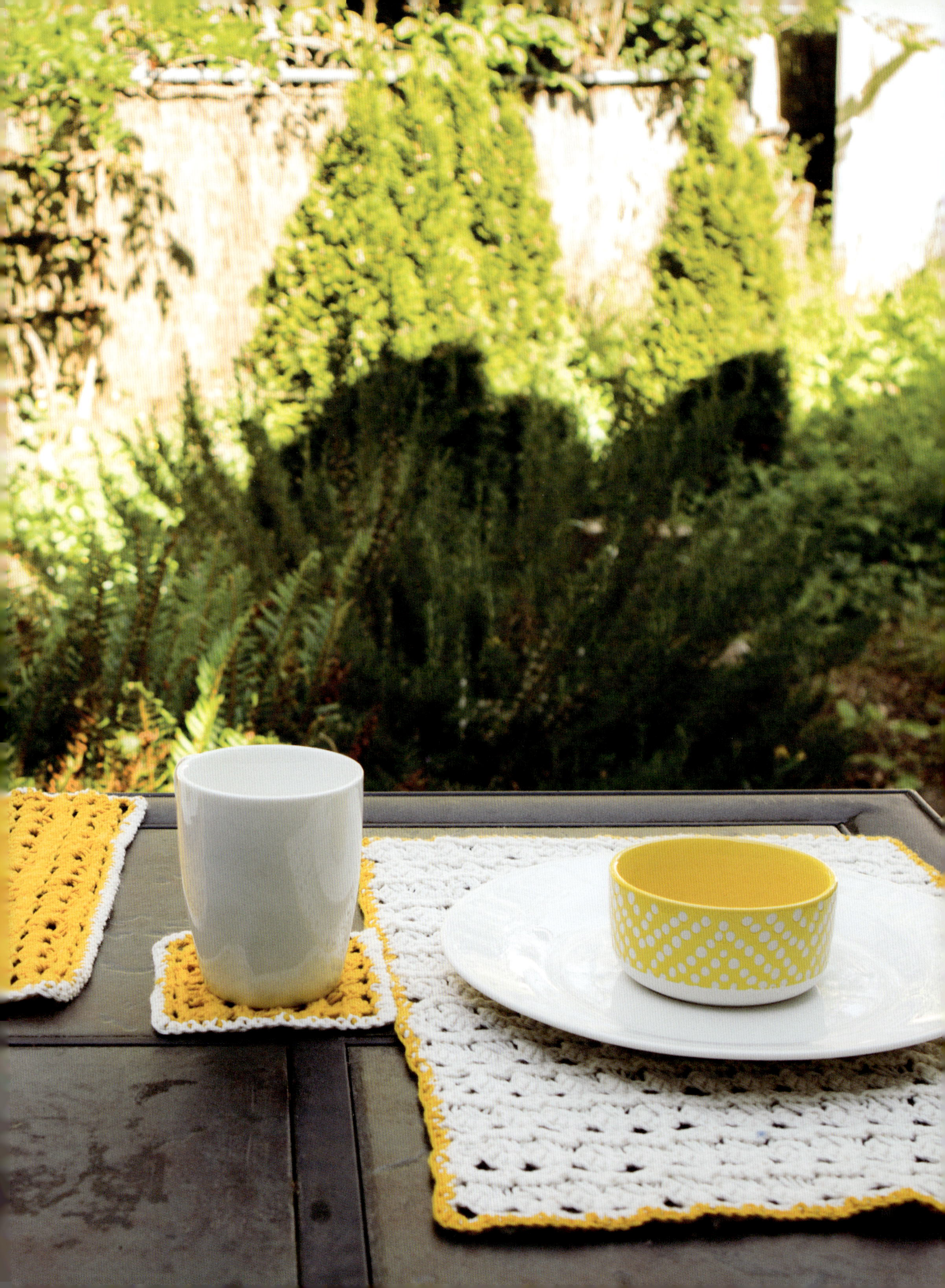

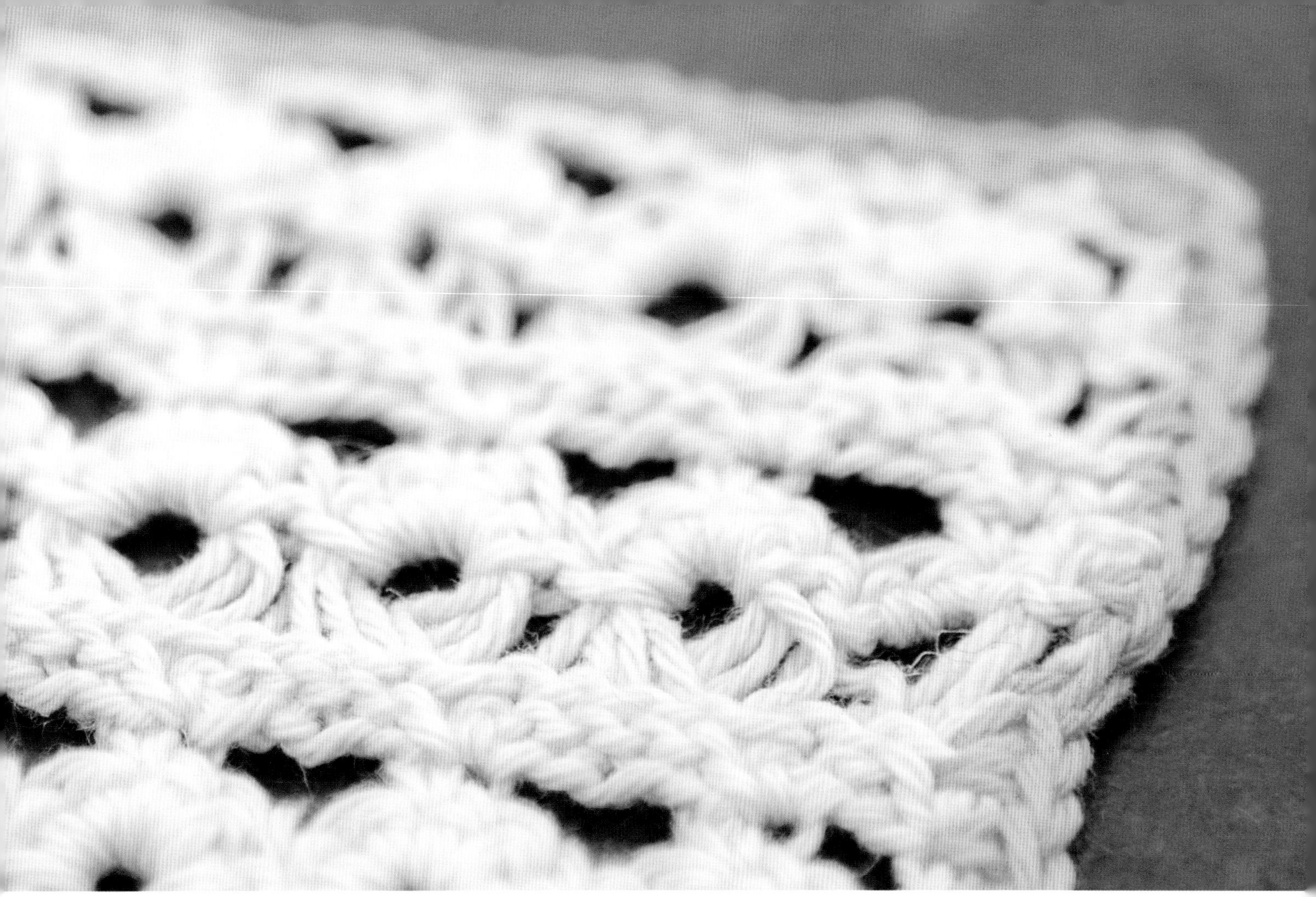

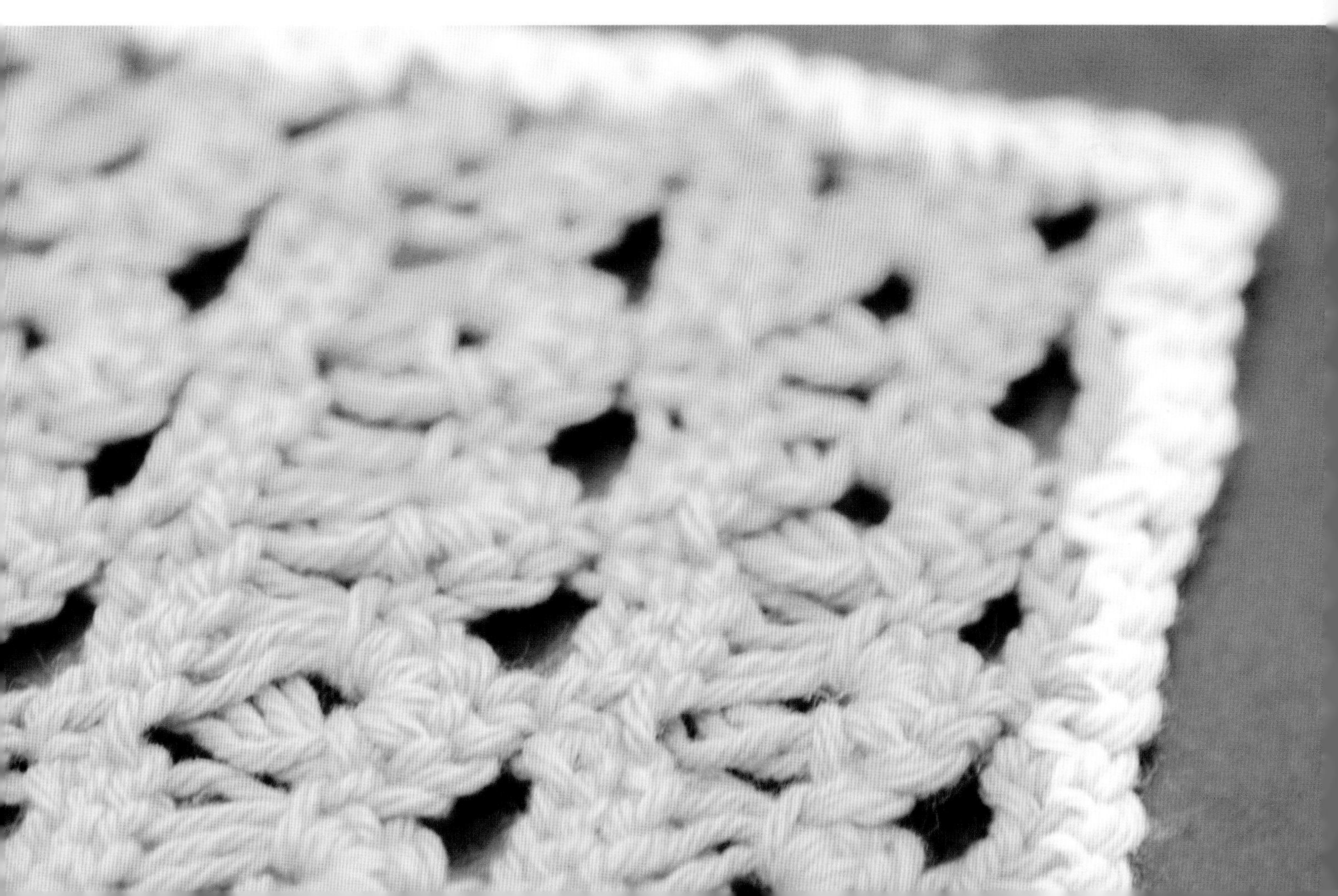

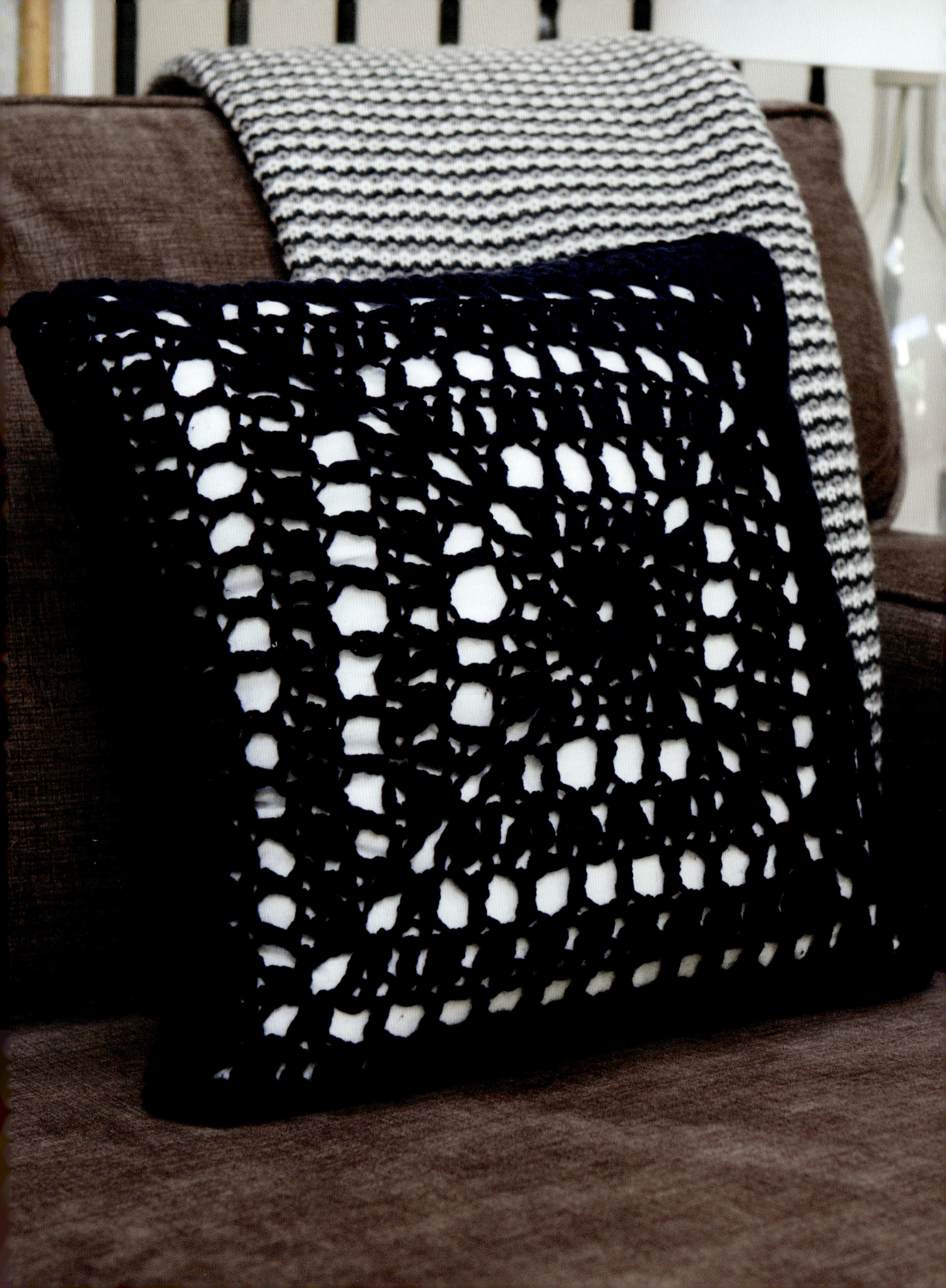

HOUSEWARMING PILLOW

by Jenni Ferwerda

FINISHED MEASUREMENTS
16" Square

YARN
Knit Picks Billow
(100% Pima Cotton; 120 yards/100g):
Navy 26983, 3 skeins.

HOOK
US N/15 (9.00 mm)

NOTIONS
Yarn Needle
6 - 1" buttons
Coordinating thread
16" square pillow form

GAUGE
9 sts and 4 rnds = 4" in stitch pattern

For pattern support, contact
jennicricket@juno.com

Notes:

The "Housewarming Pillow" is the perfect present for a newlywed couple just starting out. Soft accent pillows in various shades of blue will brighten up any room. A variation on the traditional Granny Square, the pillow is made of two squares that can be sewn together or crocheted together with a single crochet edging. The remaining edge fastens with buttons, making the crocheted shams easy to remove for washing.

DIRECTIONS

Pillow Squares

The squares are worked in the round. Make 2.

Rnd 1: Ch 4, Sl St in first ch to form a ring. Ch 3 (counts as dc), 15 DC into ring, Sl St in top of beg ch-3. 16 DC

Rnd 2: Ch 2 (counts as hdc), *HDC in next dc, [2 DC, ch 2, 2 DC] in next dc (corner made), HDC in next 2 dc; repeat from * around, ending with Sl St in top of beg ch-2. 16 dc, 12 hdc.

Rnd 3 (Eyelet Round): Ch 4 (counts as dc, ch 1), *(SK 1 st, DC in next st, ch 1) to corner ch-2 sp, [2 DC, ch 2, 2 DC] in corner ch-2 sp, ch 1; repeat from * around, ending with Sl St in 3rd ch of beg ch-4. 28 dc, 16 ch-1 spaces

Rnd 4 (Solid Round): Ch 3 (counts as dc), *DC in each dc and ch-1 sp to corner ch-2 sp, [2 DC, ch 2, 2 DC] in corner ch-2 sp; repeat from * around, ending with Sl St in top of beg ch-3. 60 dc

Rnds 5-8: Repeat Rnds 3-4 twice. 124 dc

Rnd 9: Ch 3 (counts as dc), *DC in each st to corner ch-2 sp, [2 DC, ch 2, 2 DC] in corner ch-2 sp; rep from * around, ending with Sl St in top of beg ch-3. 140 DC

Finishing

Edging

Reattach yarn to any corner ch-2 sp of first square with WS facing you, ch 1, SC 1 in ch-2 sp, SC along edge in each dc to next ch-2 sp, SC 1 in ch-2 sp.

Now lay the second square on top of the first, WS facing in and the RS of the second square facing you.

Continue around, crocheting through both layers, 2 SC in same ch-2 sp, *SC along edge in each dc to next ch-2 sp, 3 SC in next ch-2 sp; repeat from * once more, SC along edge in each dc to next ch-2 sp, 2 SC in ch-2 sp.

Now continue through only the second square, with RS facing you, SC 1 in ch-2 sp, SC in next 3 sts, ch 2, SK 1, SC in next 4 sts, ch 2, SK 1, (SC in next 5 sts, ch 2, SK 1) 3 times, SC in next 4 sts, ch 2, SK 1, SC in next 3 sts, SC 1 in ch-2 sp, Sl St to join. Fasten off.

Alternatively, sew three sides of the pillow together. Reattach yarn to ch-2 of first square on unsewn side with RS facing you. Ch 1, SC 1 in ch-2 sp, SC along edge in each dc to next ch-2 sp, SC 1 in ch-2 sp.

Turn pillow to work on 2nd square on open side. SC 1 in ch-2 sp, SC in next 3 sts, ch 2, SK 1, SC in next 4 sts, ch 2, SK 1, (SC in next 5 sts, ch 2, SK 1) 3 times, SC in next 4 sts, ch 2, SK 1, SC in next 3 sts, SC 1 in ch-2 sp, Sl St. Fasten off.

Weave in ends, wash and block to 16" square. Sew buttons in place on first square, aligning them with the buttonholes on the second square.

Legend

○ ch
Chain

T HDC
Half double crochet

╤ DC
Double crochet

Housewarming Pillow Chart

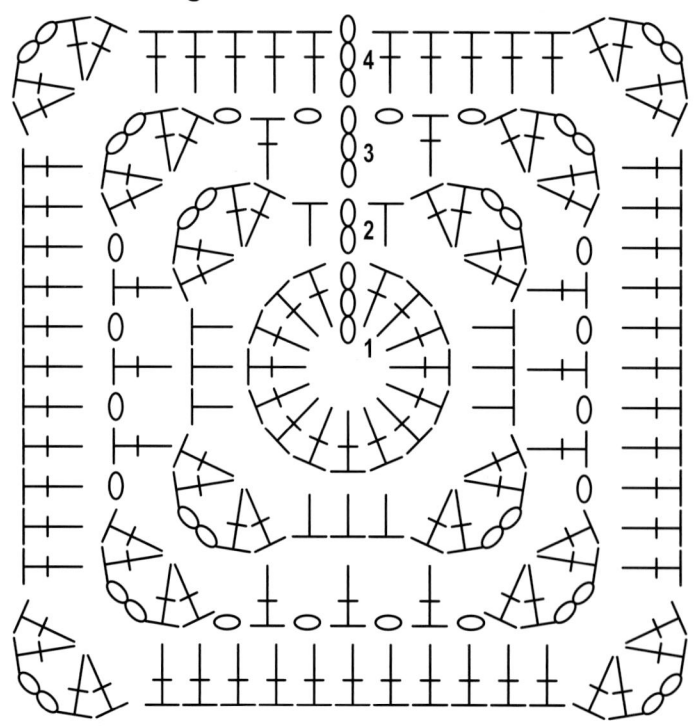

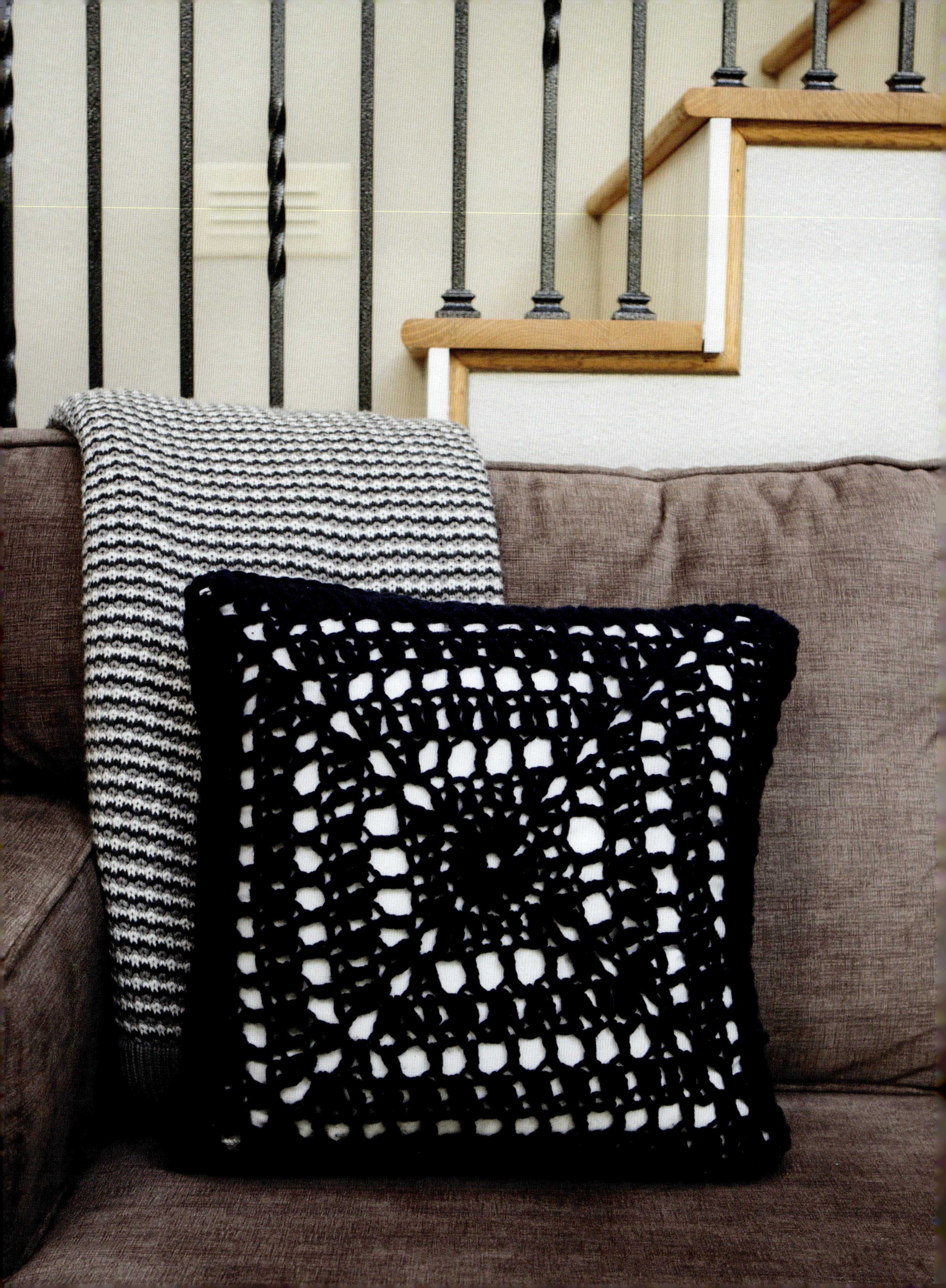

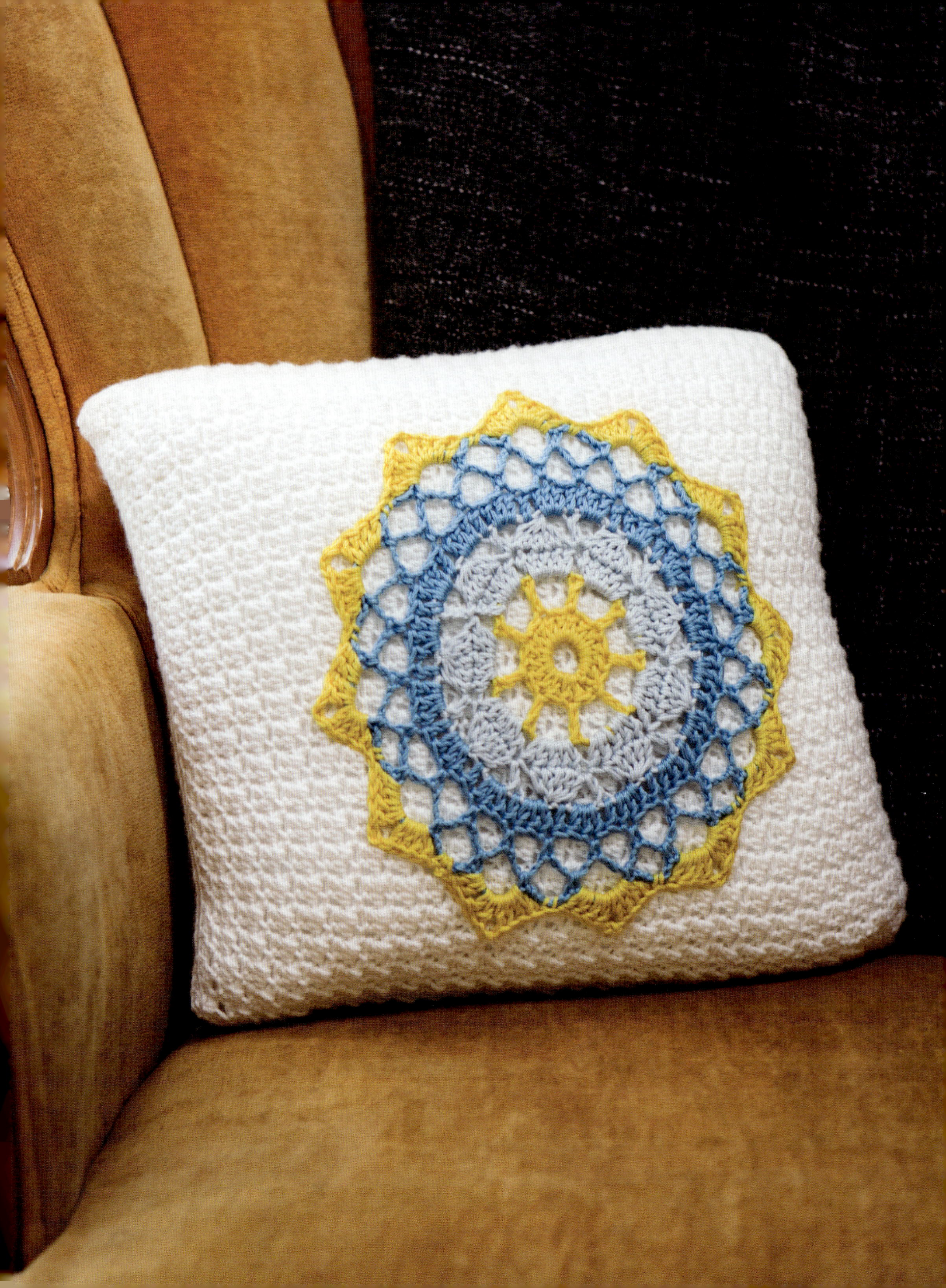

MANDALA PILLOW

by Kristi Simpson

FINISHED MEASUREMENTS
14" Square

YARN
Knit Picks Shine Sport
(60% Pima Cotton, 40% Modal®; 110 yards/50g): C1 White 24486, 3 skeins; C2 Dandelion 25340, 1 ball; C3 Clarity 26677, 1 ball; C4 Sky 23621, 1 ball.

HOOKS
US F (3.75 mm), or size to obtain gauge
US G (4.00 mm)

NOTIONS
Yarn Needle
Stitch Markers
14" x 14" pillow form

GAUGE
13 sts and 14 rows = 4", using larger hook, blocked.

For pattern support, contact
kristi.rakj@gmail.com

Mandala Pillow

Notes:
The panels are made separately and trimmed. Sew the mandala on before sewing panels together.

DC5tog: Decrease the next 5 sts together

DIRECTIONS

Panel (Make 2)
Using larger hook and C1, ch 50.
Row 1: SC in second ch from hook, *ch 1, SK 1 ch, SC in next ch; repeat from * across, turn. 49 sts
Row 2: Ch 1, SC in first st, *DC in ch-1 sp, SC in next st; repeat from * across, turn.
Row 3: Ch 1, *SC in first st, *ch 1, SK 1, SC in next st; repeat from * across, turn.
Rows 4-end: Repeat Rows 2 and 3 until panel measures 14".

Border
Working in end of rows and sts, attach C1, ch 1, evenly SC down edge around, with 3 SC in each corner, Sl St to the first st to join. Fasten off.

Mandala
The mandala is made in joined rounds.
The beginning ch-3 is the first dc of rnd.
The beginning ch-6 is the first dc + ch 3.
The beginning ch-7 is the first dc + ch 4.

Using smaller hook and C2, ch 10, Sl St to the first ch to join.
Rnd 1: Ch 3, 17 DC in ring, Sl St to beg ch-3 to join.
Rnd 2: Ch 7, *SK 1 st, DC in next st, ch 4; repeat from * around, Sl St to the first dc to join. Fasten off C2.
Rnd 3: Join C3 in any ch-4 sp, ch 3, 4 DC in same ch-4 sp, *5 DC in next ch-4 sp; repeat from * around, Sl St to the first dc to join.
Rnd 4: Ch 6, using the same st as first dc, DC5tog, ch 3, *DC in next st, using same st as dc, ch 3, DC5tog, ch 3; repeat from * around, Sl St to the first dc to join. Fasten off C3.
Rnd 5: Join C4, ch 3, *DC 3 in ch-3 sp, DC in top of dc5tog st, DC 3 in ch-3 sp, **DC in next st; repeat from * around, ending at **, Sl St to beg ch-3 to join.
Rnd 6: Ch 1, SC in same st, *ch 5, SK 2 sts, SC in next; repeat from * around to last 2 sts, ch 3, DC in first st to join.
Rnd 7: Sl St in next ch-5 sp, ch 1, SC in same sp, *ch 5, SC in next ch-5 sp; repeat from * around to last ch-sp, ch 2, DC to first sc to join. Fasten off.
Rnd 8: Join C2 in first st, ch 1, SC in same st, [4 DC, ch 3, 4 DC] in next ch-5 sp, *SC in next ch-5 sp, [4 DC, ch 3, 4 DC] in next ch-5 sp; repeat from * around, Sl St to the first st to join. Fasten off.

Finishing
Weave in ends, wash, and block panels to measurements.
Use yarn needle to sew onto panel.
Sew panels together around pillow form.

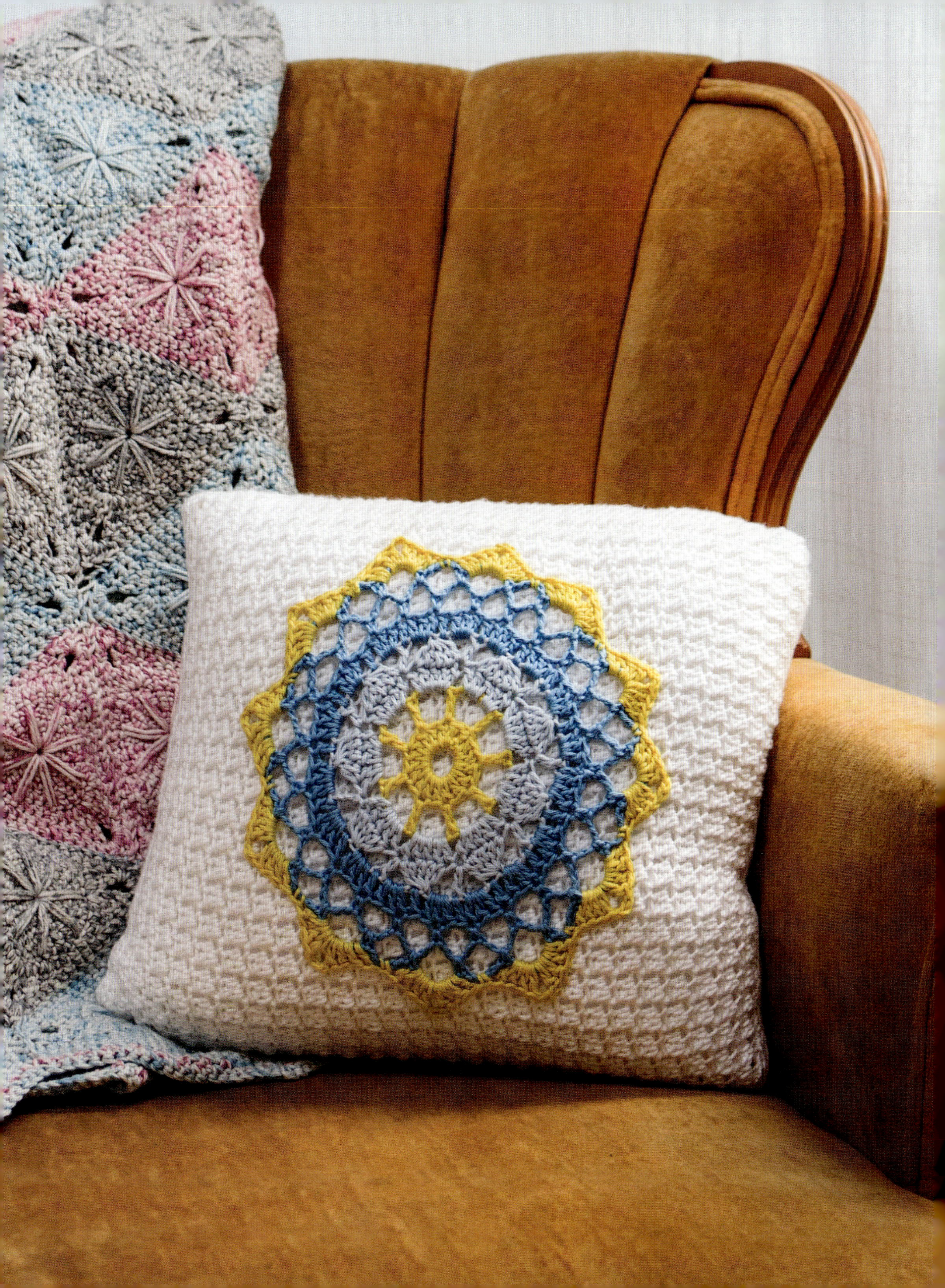

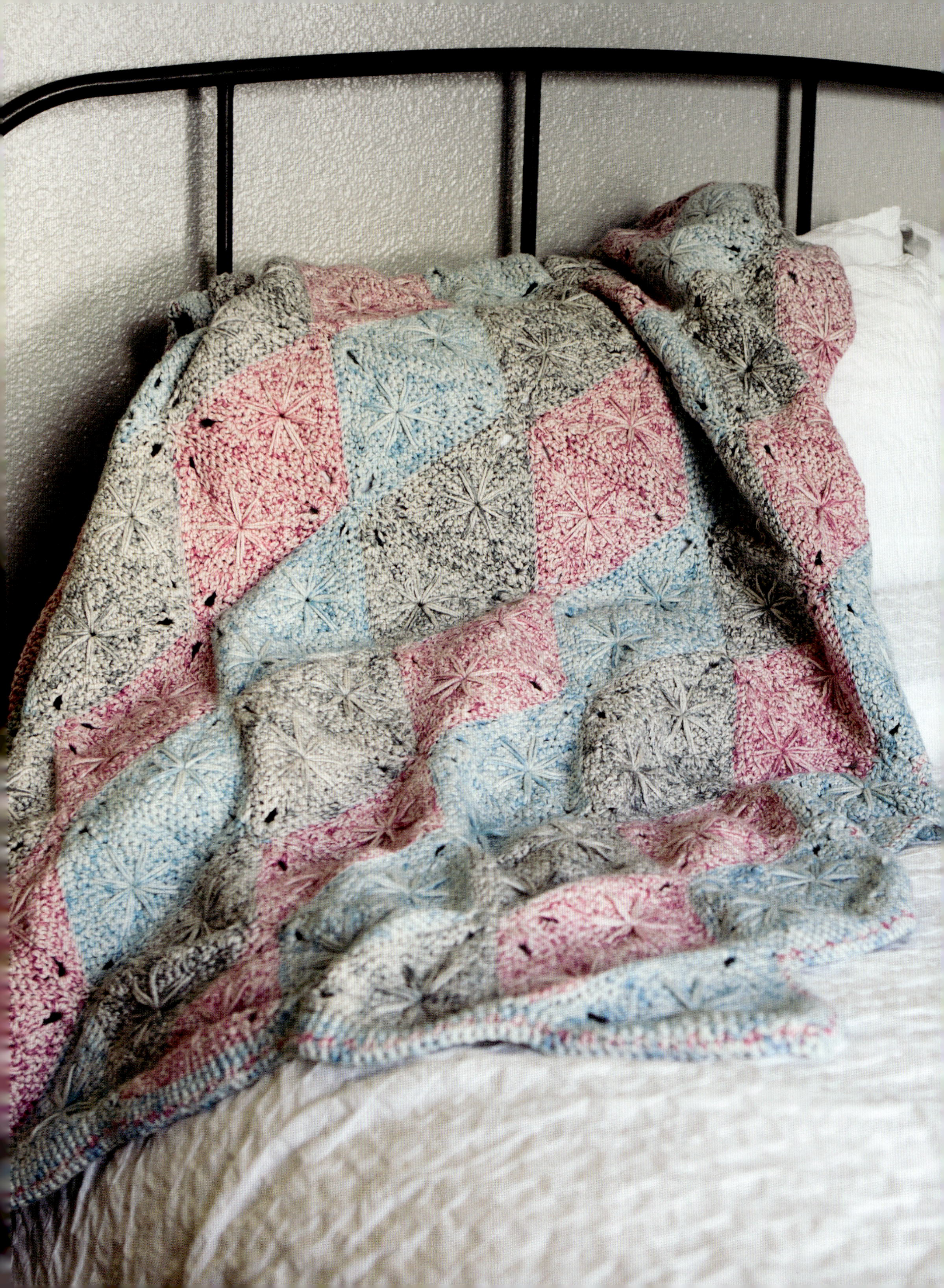

SERENITY AFGHAN

by Kristen Stoltzfus Clay

FINISHED MEASUREMENTS
37" x 53"

YARN
Knit Picks Color Mist
(75% Pima Cotton, 25% Acrylic; 219 yards/100g): C1 Cloudburst 27458, 6 skeins; C2 Dahlia 27461, 4 skeins; C3 Tidewater 27465, 4 skeins.

HOOKS
US G/6 (4.00 mm)

NOTIONS
Yarn Needle
Stitch Markers

GAUGE
Motif: 5" tip to tip, 4.25" across from side to tip; blocked.

For pattern support, contact
joysinstitches@outlook.com

Notes:
Like leaves floating in ripples on a pool of water, the Serenity Afghan features individual motifs that blossom from a circle into a triangle with a star center formed by long single crochet stitches. The soothing three tone color palette, triangle and diamond motifs, and shaped sides make it special but the motifs are easy to do and are a great tote-along project.

Long single crochet (Long SC): Insert hook in center hole, draw up a new lp over the previous 4 rnds as high as working rnd, complete sc. Do not pull too snugly.

Single crochet 3 together (SC3tog): (Insert hook in specified st, draw up a lp) 3 times, draw new lp through all 4 lps on hook.

DIRECTIONS

Motif (make 60 in C1, 48 in C2, 48 in C3)
Ch 4, join with Sl St in first sc to form ring.
Rnd 1: Ch 1, work 8 SC in ring, do not join (use stitch markers if desired to keep track of beginning of rnd). 8 sc
Rnd 2: (2 SC in next sc) around, do not join. 16 sc
Rnd 3: (SC in next sc, 2 SC in next SC) around, do not join. 24 sc
Rnd 4: SC in each sc around, do not join.
Rnd 5: (SC in each of next 2 sc, work Long SC, 2 SC in sc behind long sc) around, join with Sl St in first long sc. 32 sc, 8 long sc
Rnd 6: (Ch 1, SC) in first st, *SC in each of next 2 sts, HDC in next st, DC in each of next 2 sts, 2 TR in next st, ch 2, 2 TR in next st, DC in each of next 2 sts, HDC in next st, SC in each of next 3 sts; rep from * around, omit last sc, SK last st, join with Sl St in first sc. 15 sc, 6 hdc, 12 dc, 12 tr, 3 ch-2 sps
Rnd 7: (Ch 1, SC) in first st, *work 1 SC in each st to corner ch-2 sp, in ch-2 sp work (2 HDC, DC, 2 HDC); rep from * around, work 1 SC in each rem st, join with Sl St in first sc. Fasten off.

Assembly
Weave in ends. Sew motifs together in back lps only following Assembly Diagram.

Edging
With RS facing, join C1 in corner to work across short end.
Rnd 1: **(SC in each sc and hdc of motif side, HDC in dc at tip where it is sewn to next motif, 2 DC in tip of inverted motif, HDC in dc at tip of next motif) across short end, SC in each sc and hdc of last motif, work (SC, ch 2, SC) in dc at corner, turn to work up long side; *SC in each sc and hdc of motif side, work SC3tog over tips of joining 3 motifs, SC in each sc and hdc of next motif, (HDC, DC, HDC) in next joining seam; rep from * across long side, ending with SC in each sc and hdc of last motif side, work (SC, ch 2, SC) in dc at corner. Rep from ** once more, join with Sl St in first sc.
Rnd 2: *SC in each st across short end, working (SC, ch 2, SC) in ch-2 sp at corner, to work across long side [work SC in each of next 20 sc, work SC3tog in next (sc, sc3tog, and sc), SC in each of next 20 sts, 3 SC in next dc] across long side, SC in each of next 20 sc, work SC3tog in next (sc, sc3tog, and sc), SC in each of next 20 sts, work (SC, ch 2, SC) in ch-2 sp at corner. Rep from * once more, join with Sl St in first sc. Fasten off C1.
Rnd 3: Join C2 in corner ch-2 sp to work across short end, *work (SC, HDC, SC) in corner sp, ch 1, SK next sc, (SC in next sc, ch 1, SK next sc) across, work (SC, HDC, SC) in corner sp, ch 1, [(SK next sc, SC in next sc, ch 1) to sc3tog, Sl St in sc3tog, ch 1, (SK next sc, SC in next sc, ch 1) 10 times, SK next sc, HDC in next sc, ch 1] across long side, (SK next sc, SC in next sc, ch 1) to last sc3tog, Sl St in sc3tog, ch 1, (SK next sc, SC in next sc, ch 1) to corner sp. Rep from * once more, join with Sl St in first sc. Fasten off C2.
Rnd 4: Join C1 in corner hdc to work across short end, *work (SC, HDC, SC) in corner hdc, SC in each st across short end to corner hdc, work (SC, HDC, SC) in corner hdc, SC in each of next 21 sts, [SK next (ch-1 sp, sl st, and ch-1 sp), SC in next 20 sts, work (SC, ch 1, SC) in next hdc, SC in each of next 20 sts] across long side, SK next (ch-1 sp, sl st, and ch-1 sp), SC in each rem st to corner hdc. Rep from * once more, join with Sl St in first sc. Fasten off.

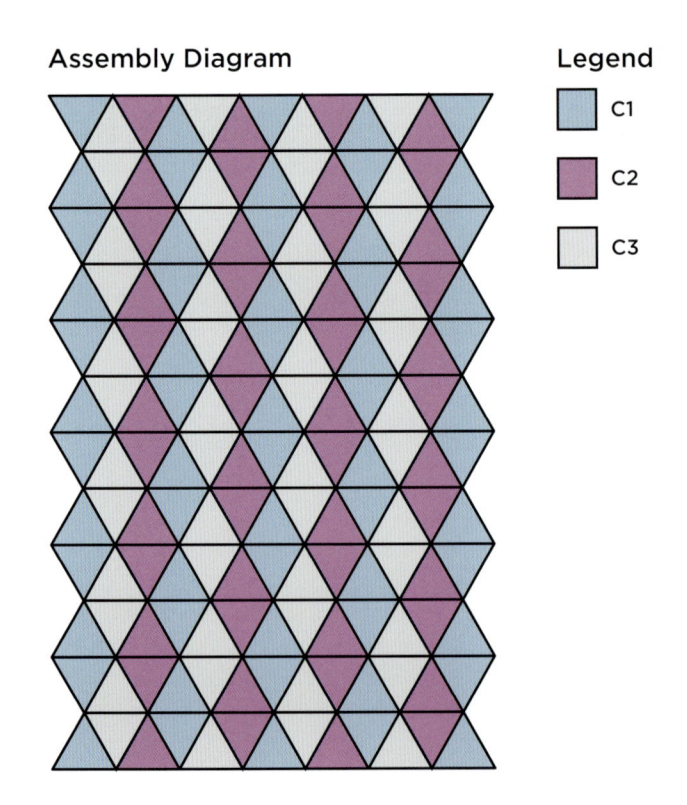

Assembly Diagram

Legend
- C1
- C2
- C3

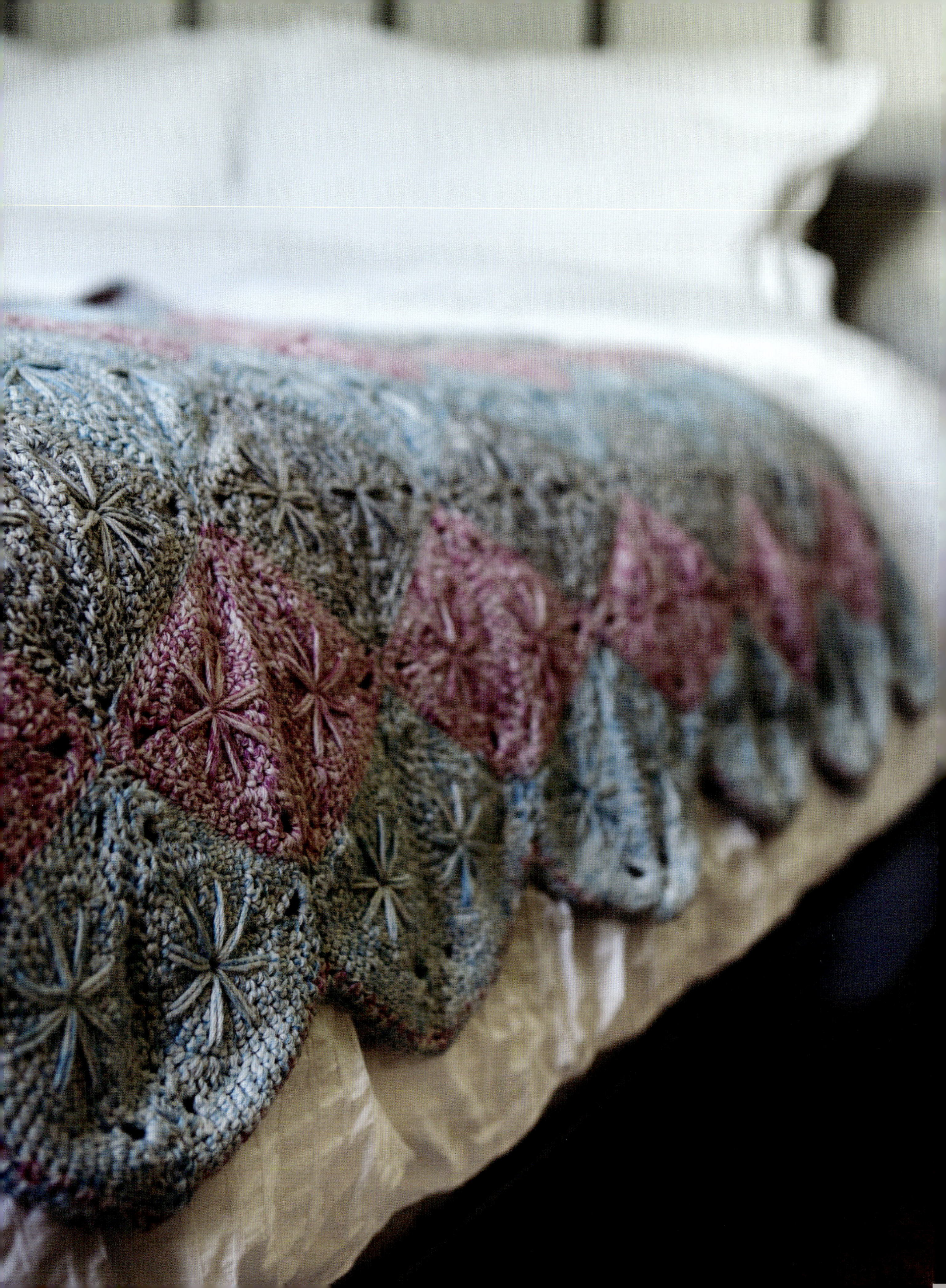

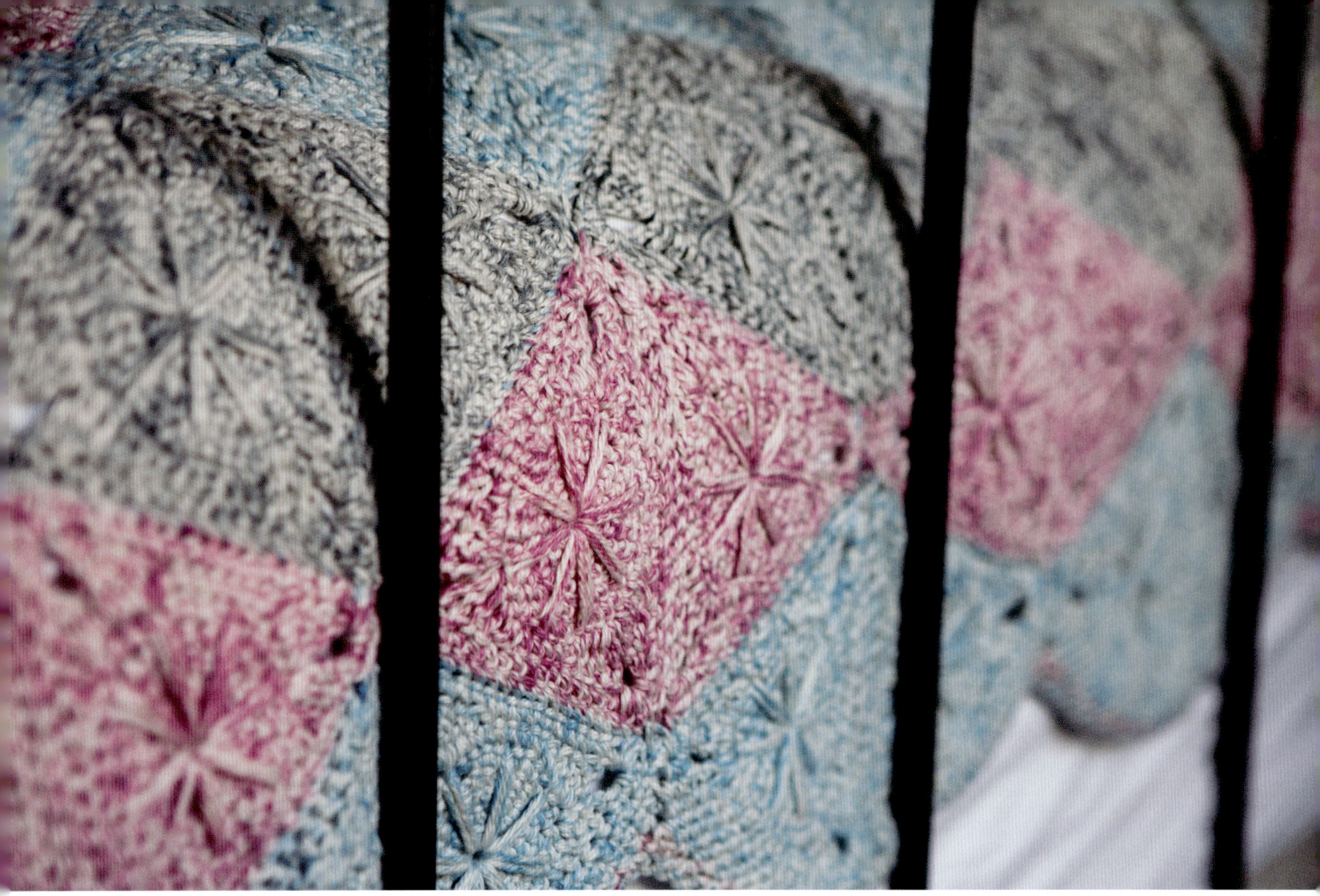

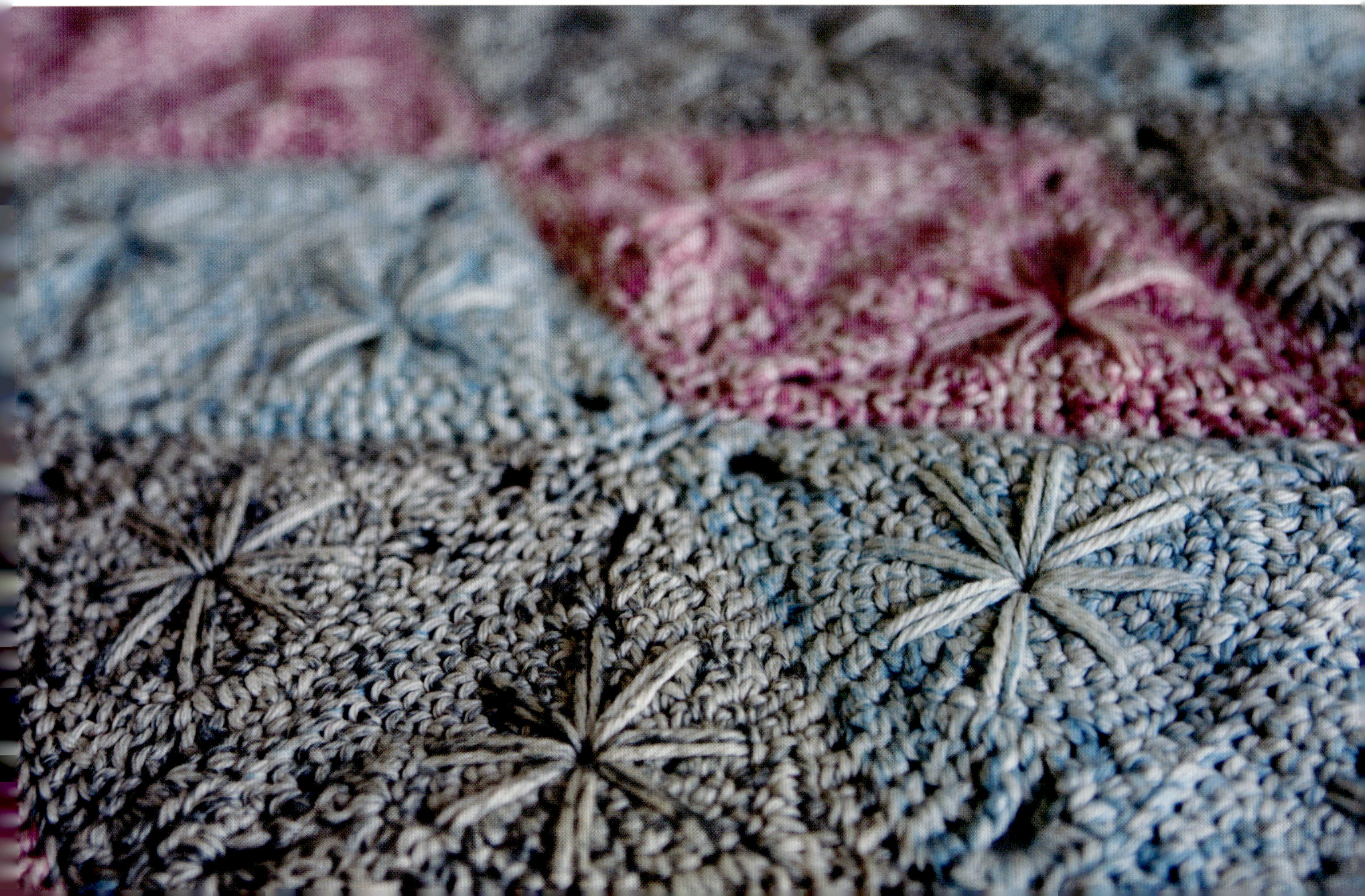

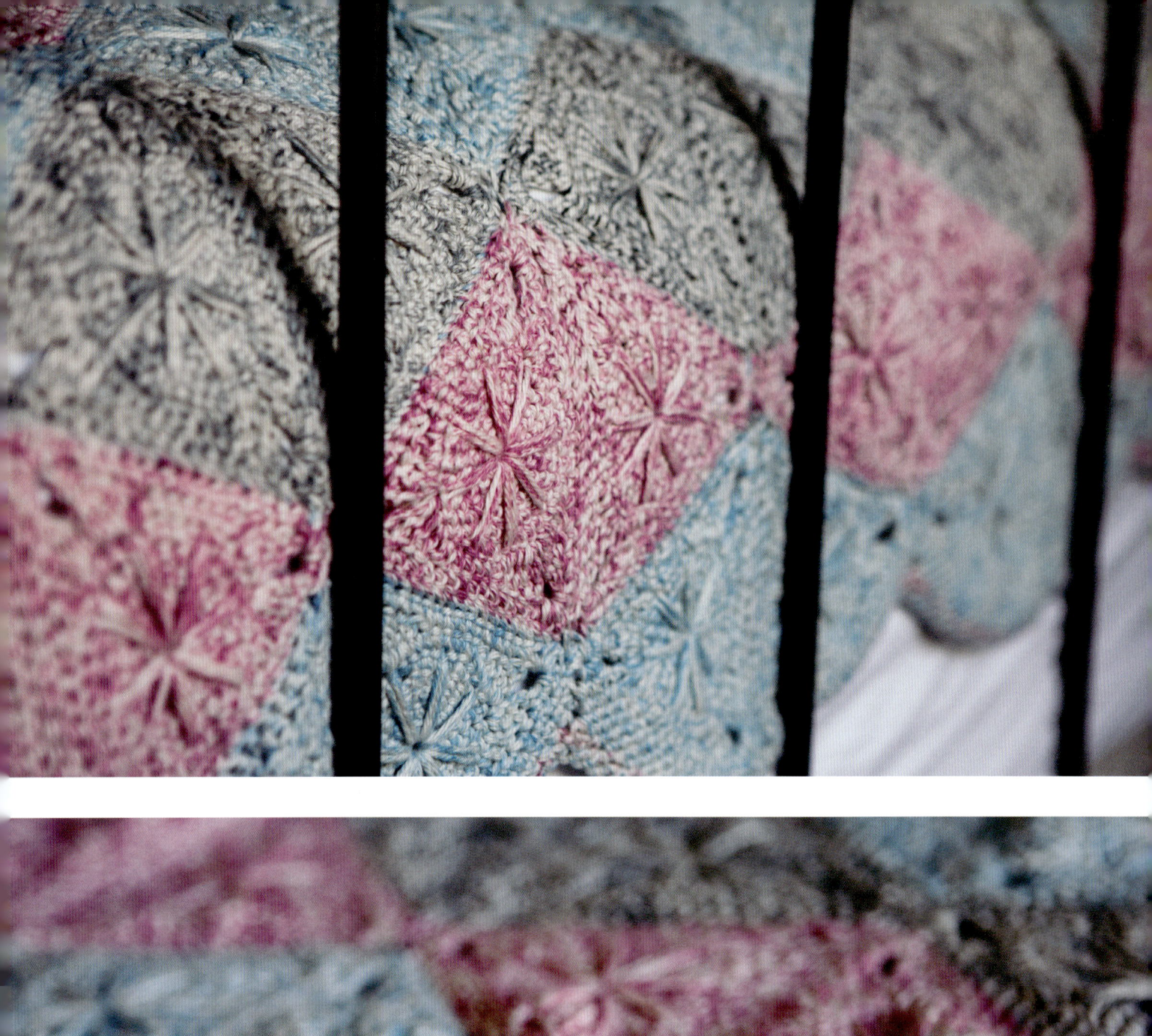

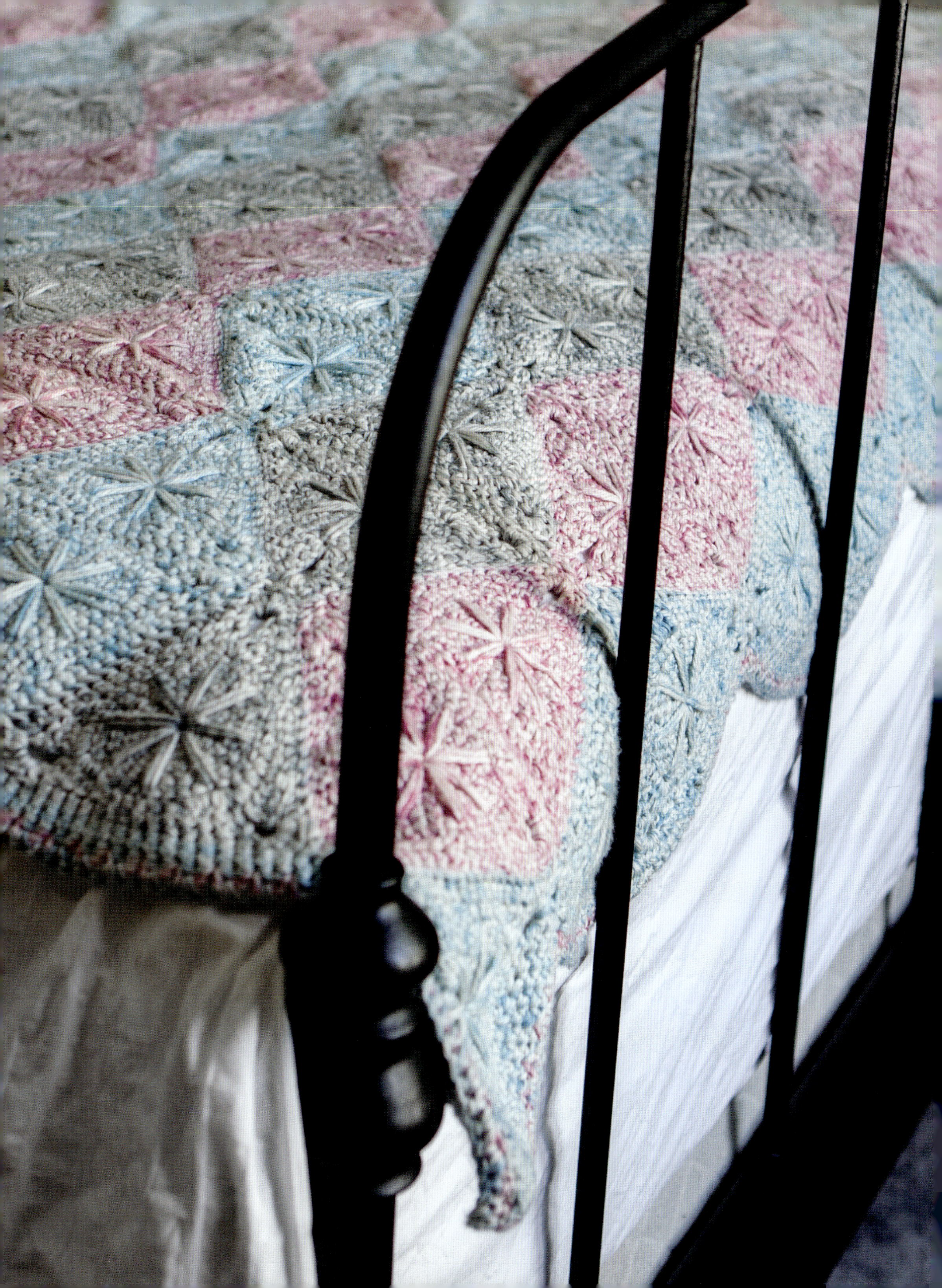

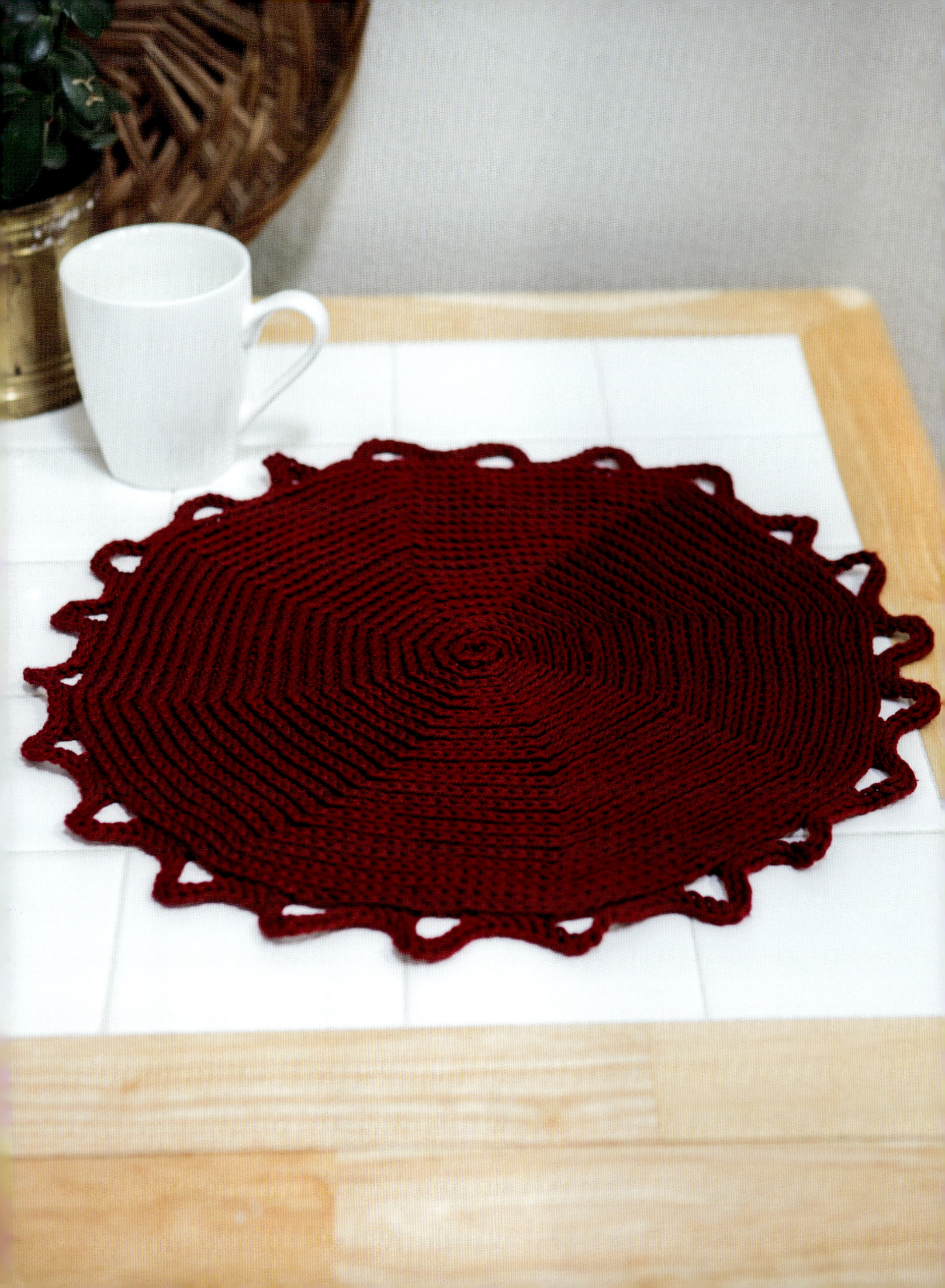

TIDEPOOL PLACEMAT

by Sharon Ballsmith

FINISHED MEASUREMENTS
Placemat: 15.5" Diameter, blocked
Plant Mat: 9.25" Diameter, blocked
Large Center Table Mat: 20" Diameter, blocked
Coaster: 5.5" Diameter, blocked

YARN
Knit Picks Comfy Worsted
(75% Pima Cotton, 25% Acrylic; 109 yards/50g): Hollyberry 26981, Placemat: 2 balls; Plant Mat: 1 ball; Large Center Table Mat: 3 balls; Coaster: 1 ball.

HOOKS
US H/8 (5.00 mm), or size to obtain gauge.

NOTIONS
Yarn Needle
Removable Stitch Marker

GAUGE
Rnds 1-6 = 4" diameter, blocked.

For pattern support, contact
stitchesandstones@email.com

Notes:

Tidepool is relaxing and easy-to-make, featuring simple textured lines juxtaposed with a playful curvy border. Tidepool is worked in the round, with an easy-to-memorize stitch pattern, from the center out towards the border. Each rnd is worked with right side facing throughout pattern in a continuous spiral, with no turning and no joining after each rnd.

Horizontal bar-Half Double Crochet (hb-HDC):
Reaching over top edge of piece to the reverse side, YO, insert hook in horizontal bar behind the hdc of previous rnd, YO and pull up a lp, YO and draw through all 3 lps on hook. (This horizontal bar can also be referred to as the "hidden third lp" of a HDC.)

Increase (INC)
2 hb-HDC in place indicated.

Horizontal bar-Single Crochet (hb-SC)
Reaching over top edge of piece to the reverse side, YO, insert hook in horizontal bar behind the hdc of previous rnd, YO and draw through both lps on hook.

Place Marker (PM)
PM in last st after completing rnd, RM as you come to it and replace it after working st, moving it up on each rnd.

DIRECTIONS

Placemat
Rnd 1: Ch 2, 8 HDC in 2nd ch from hook, PM. 8 HDC
Rnd 2: INC in each next 8 HDC, PM. 16 hb-HDC
Rnd 3: *1 hb-HDC in next st, INC in next st; repeat from * around to first st, PM. 24 hb-HDC
Rnd 4: *1 hb-HDC in each next 2 sts, INC in next st; repeat from * around to first st, PM. 32 hb-HDC
Rnd 5: *1 hb-HDC in each next 3 sts, INC in next st; repeat from * around to first st, PM. 40 hb-HDC
Rnds 6-22: Continue working in the same manner by adding 1 more hb-HDC before the inc in each repeat (this will add 8 more sts evenly around on each consecutive rnd). 176 hb-HDC after completing Rnd 22

Placemat Border
Row 1: 1 hb-HDC in each hb-HDC around, PM. 176 hb-HDC
Row 2: *1 hb-SC in each next 5 hb-HDC, ch 8, SK 3 hb-HDC; repeat from * around. 110 hb-SC, 22 ch-8 lps
Row 3: Sl St BLO in each hb-SC and ch-st around, join with Sl St to first sl st. 286 sl sts
Fasten off.

Plant Mat
Rnd 1: Ch 2, 8 HDC in 2nd ch from hook, PM. 8 HDC
Rnd 2: INC in each next 8 HDC, PM. 16 hb-HDC
Rnd 3: *1 hb-HDC in next st, INC in next st; repeat from * around to first st, PM. 24 hb-HDC
Rnd 4: *1 hb-HDC in each next 2 sts, INC in next st; repeat from * around to first st, PM. 32 hb-HDC
Rnd 5: *1 hb-HDC in each next 3 sts, INC in next st; repeat from * around up to first st, PM. 40 hb-HDC
Rnds 6-11: Continue working in the same manner by adding 1 more hb-HDC before the inc in each repeat (this will add 8 more sts evenly around on each consecutive rnd). 88 hb-HDC after completing Rnd 11

Plant Mat Border
Row 1: 1 hb-HDC in each hb-HDC around, PM. 88 hb-HDC
Row 2: *1 hb-SC in each next 5 hb-HDC, ch 8, SK 3 hb-HDC; repeat from * around. 55 hb-SC, 11 ch-8 lps
Row 3: Sl St BLO in each hb-SC and ch-st around, join with Sl St to first sl st. 143 sl sts
Fasten off.

Large Center Table Mat
Rnd 1: Ch 2, 8 HDC in 2nd ch from hook, PM. 8 HDC
Rnd 2: INC in each next 8 HDC, PM. 16 hb-HDC
Rnd 3: *1 hb-HDC in next st, INC in next st; repeat from * around to first st, PM. 24 hb-HDC
Rnd 4: *1 hb-HDC in each next 2 sts, INC in next st; repeat from * around to first st, PM. 32 hb-HDC
Rnd 5: *1 hb-HDC in each next 3 sts, INC in next st; repeat from * around to first st, PM. 40 hb-HDC
Rnds 6-27: Continue working in the same manner by adding 1 more hb-HDC before the inc in each repeat (this will add 8 more sts evenly around on each consecutive rnd). 216 hb-HDC after completing Rnd 27

Large Center Table Mat Border
Row 1: 1 hb-HDC in each hb-HDC around, PM. 216 hb-HDC
Row 2: *1 hb-SC in each next 5 hb-HDC, ch 8, SK 3 hb-HDC; repeat from * around. 135 hb-SC, 27 ch-8 lps
Row 3: Sl St BLO in each hb-SC and ch-st around, join with Sl St to first sl st. 351 sl sts
Fasten off.

Coaster
Rnd 1: Ch 2, 8 HDC in 2nd ch from hook, PM. 8 HDC
Rnd 2: INC in each next 8 HDC, PM. 16 hb-HDC
Rnd 3: *1 hb-HDC in next st, INC in next st; repeat from * around to first st, PM. 24 hb-HDC
Rnd 4: *1 hb-HDC in each next 2 sts, INC in next st; repeat from * around to first st, PM. 32 hb-HDC
Rnd 5: *1 hb-HDC in each next 3 sts, INC in next st; repeat from * around to first st, PM. 40 hb-HDC

Coaster Border
Row 1: 1 hb-HDC in each hb-HDC around, PM. 40 hb-HDC
Row 2: *1 hb-SC in each next 3 hb-HDC, ch 8, SK 2 hb-HDC; repeat from * around. 24 hb-SC, 8 ch-8 lps
Row 3: Sl St BLO in each hb-SC and ch-st around, join with Sl St to first sl st. 88 sl sts
Fasten off.

Finishing
Weave in ends. Block to measurements, if desired.

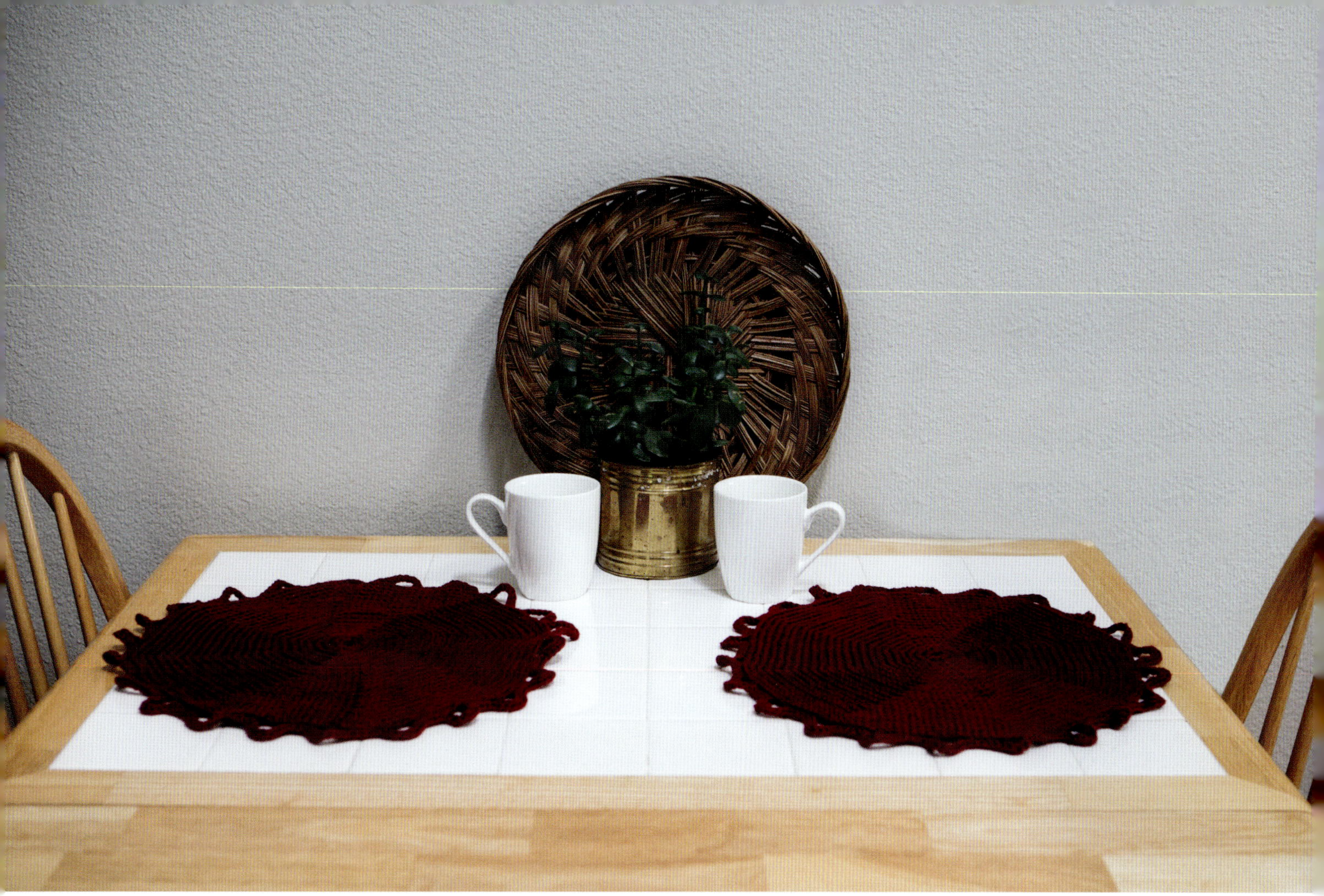
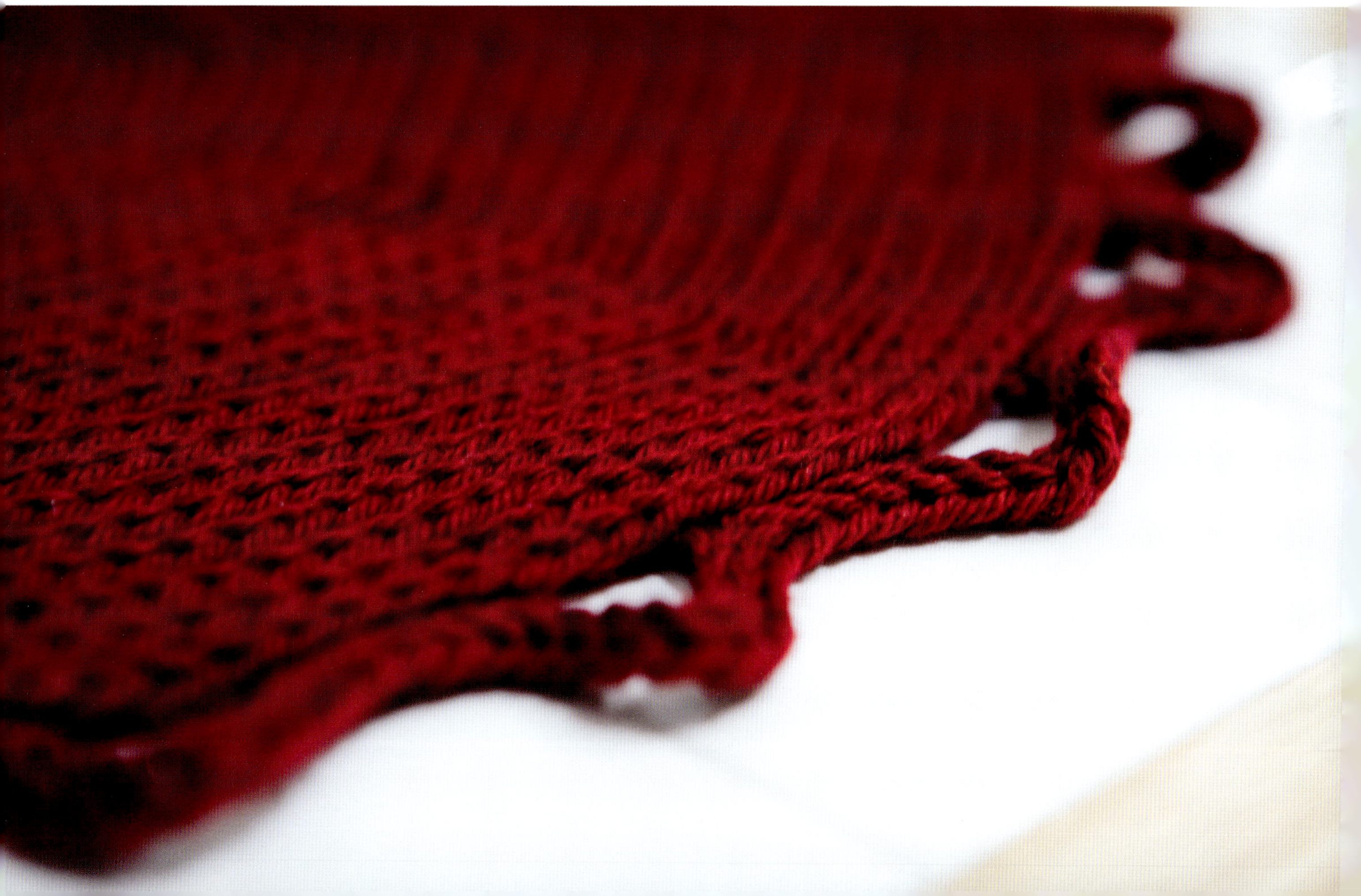

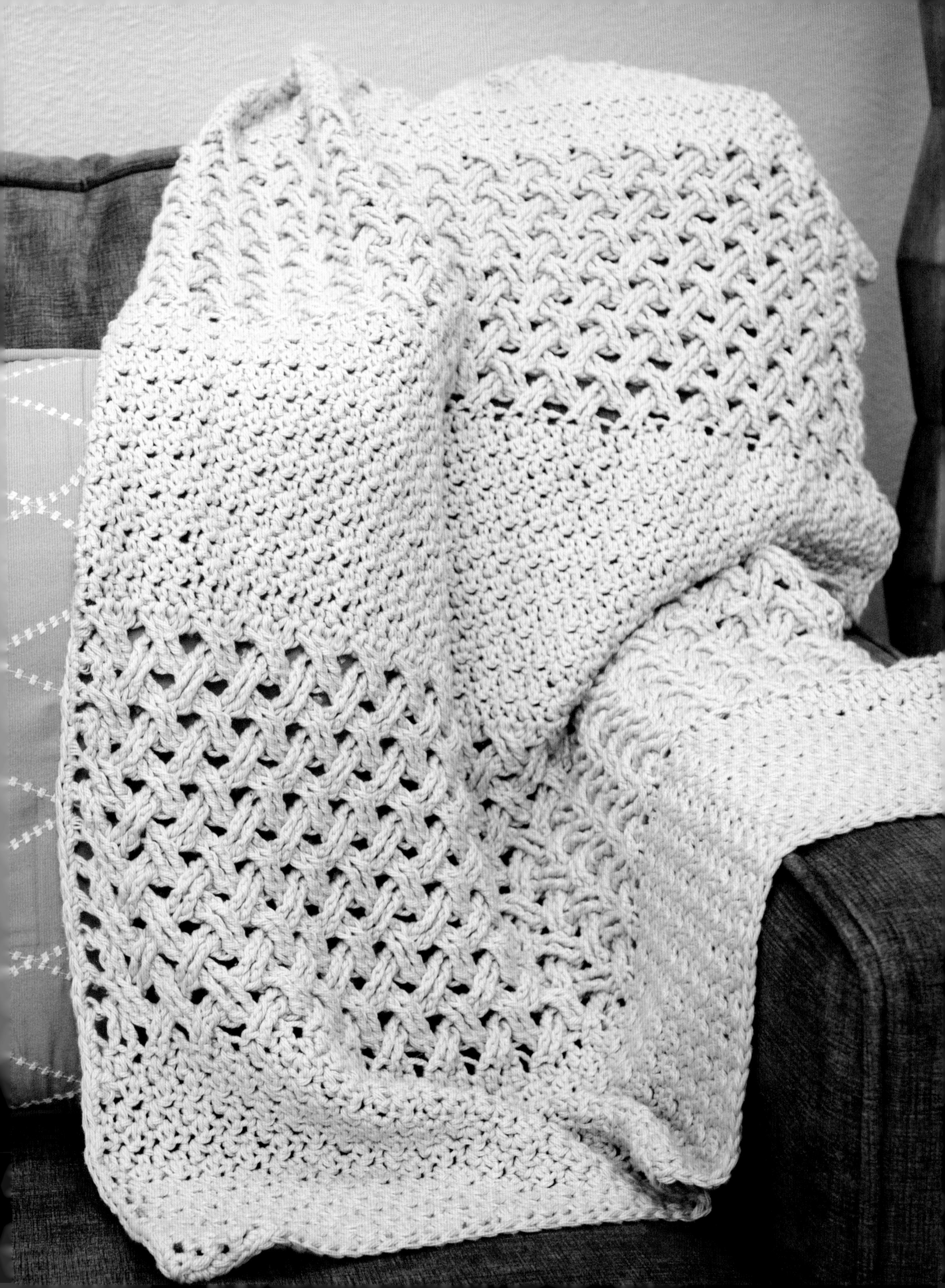

WOVEN BLANKET

by Kristi Simpson

FINISHED MEASUREMENTS
30" x 50"

YARN
Knit Picks Comfy Worsted
(75% Pima Cotton, 25% Acrylic; 109 yards/50g): Silver Sage 24424, 12 balls.

HOOKS
US H/8 (5.00 mm), or size to obtain gauge

GAUGE
12 sts and 14 rows = 4" in (sc, dc) pattern, blocked.

For pattern support, contact
kristi.rakj@gmail.com

Notes:
Cuddle your sweet one in softness and texture. It is a stunning blanket that mixes stitches to create a unique woven look. Don't be afraid of the texture, it is just as easy as counting your stitches. The beautiful blanket will create a priceless heirloom for years to come.

The beginning ch-3 will be the first dc of row unless otherwise noted.

DIRECTIONS

Blanket
Ch 79.

Row 1: SC in second ch from hook, DC in next ch, *SC in next ch, DC in next ch; repeat from * across, turn. 78 sts

Rows 2-19: Ch 1, *SC in next st, DC in next st; repeat from * across, turn.

Row 20: Ch 3, *SK 2 sts, FPtr in next 2 sts, working over the last 2 sts, FPtr in first skipped st, FPtr in second skipped st; repeat from * across, DC in last st, turn.

Row 21: Ch 3, BPtr in next 2 sts, *SK 2 sts, BPtr in next 2 sts, working behind last 2 sts, BPtr in first skipped stitch, BPtr in second skipped stitch; repeat from * across to last 3 sts, BPtr in next 2 sts, DC in last st, turn.
Rows 22-31: Repeat Rows 20 and 21.
Rows 32-49: Repeat Row 2.
Rows 50-61: Repeat Rows 20 and 21.
Rows 62-79: Repeat Row 2.
Rows 80-91: Repeat Rows 20 and 21.
Rows 92-109: Repeat Row 2. Fasten off.

Border
Working in ends of rows and sts, attach yarn, ch 1, evenly SC down edge around, with 3 SC in each corner, Sl St to the first st to join. Fasten off.

Finishing
Weave in ends, wash and block to measurements.

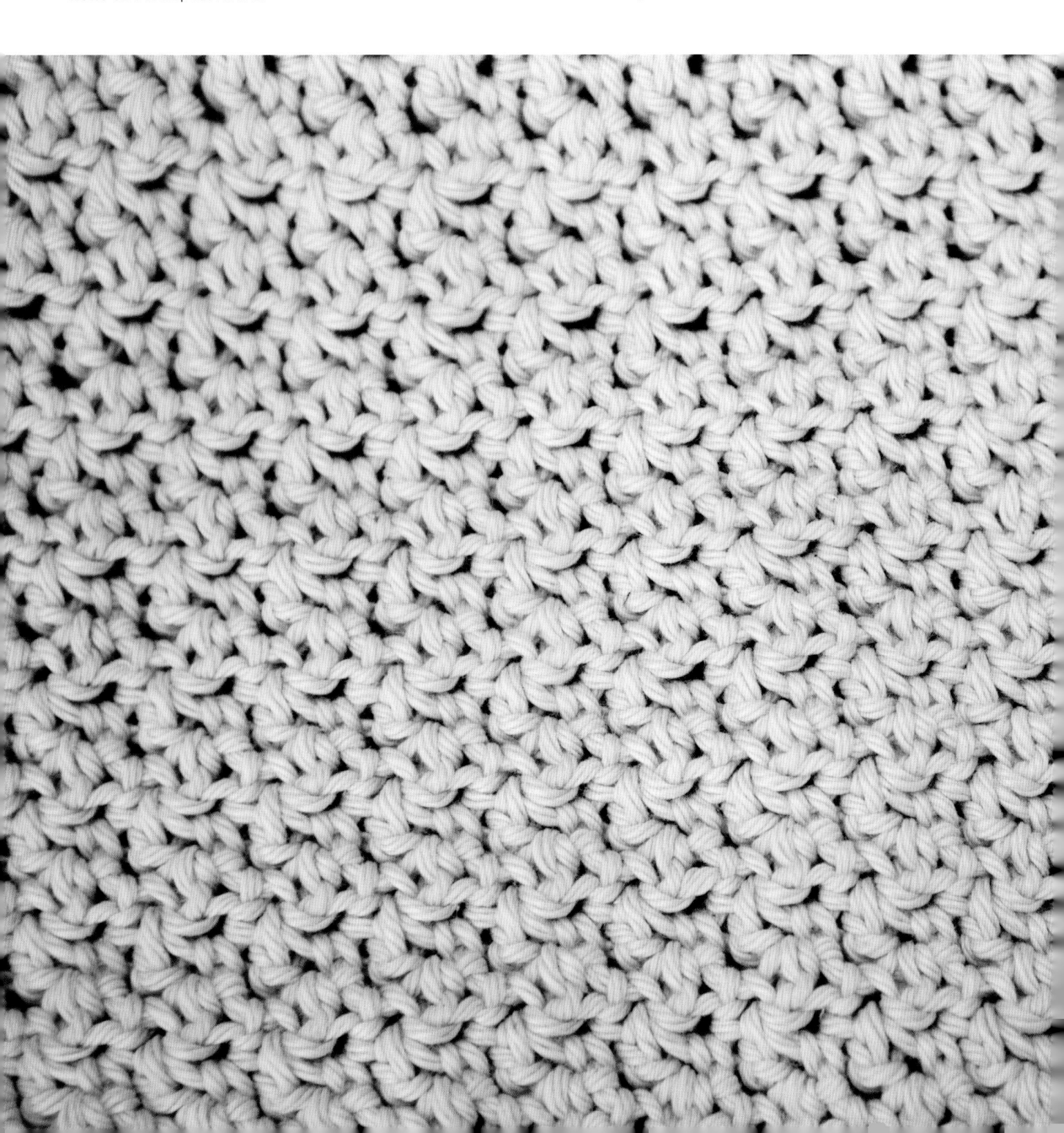

Crochet Abbreviations

beg	beginning	FPtr	front post treble	shell	a group of stitches all worked in the same stitch
Blp	single or double crochet in back loop only	HDC	half double crochet	sk	skip
		lp(s)	loop(s)	sl	slip
BPDC	back post double crochet	MC	main color	sl st	slip stitch
BPtr	back post treble	PM	place marker	st(s)	stitch(es)
C (1, 2...)	color (1, 2...)	rem	remaining	tr	treble crochet
ch(s)	chain(s)	rep	repeat	Tch	top of turning chain made at start of previous row
ch-sp	chain space	RM	remove marker		
DC	double crochet	rnd(s)	round(s)	WS	wrong side
FSC	foundation single crochet	RS	right side	YO	yarn over
FPDC	front post double crochet	SC	single crochet	**	repeat directions given from * to *
		SC2tog	single crochet two together		

Knit Picks yarn is both luxe and affordable—a seeming contradiction trounced! But it's not just about the pretty colors; we also care deeply about fiber quality and fair labor practices, leaving you with a gorgeously reliable product you'll turn to time and time again.

THIS COLLECTION FEATURES

Shine
Sport Weight
60% Pima Cotton,
40% Modal® natural beech wood fiber

CotLin
DK Weight
70% Tanguis Cotton,
30% Linen

Color Mist
Worsted Weight
75% Pima Cotton,
25% Acrylic

Comfy
Worsted Weight
75% Pima Cotton,
25% Acrylic

Billow
Bulky Weight
100% Pima Cotton

View these beautiful yarns and more at www.KnitPicks.com